THE
HINDU HISTORY OF KASHMIR

THE
HINDU HISTORY OF KASHMIR

by

H. H. WILSON

GYAN

Published by

GYAN

Gyan Publishing House
5, Ansari Road
Daryaganj, New Delhi-110002
Phone: 011-47034999, 9811692060
E-mail: books@gyanbooks.com

Distribution Network
gyanbooks.com
India, USA, Canada, UK, Australia

ISBN: 978-81-212-7019-9 (PB)
First Published, 1860

2nd Impression 2024

Printed at: Gyan Press, Delhi.

THE HINDU HISTORY OF KASHMIR
Author: H. H. WILSON

THE
HINDU HISTORY OF KASHMIR

THE
HINDU HISTORY OF KASHMIR

by

H. H. WILSON

CONTENTS

PUBLISHERS' NOTE

This volume is made up of three papers on the history and chronology of Kashmir based on Kalhana's great Sanskrit Kavya *Rajatarangini,* which contains nearly 8000 *slokas.* Besides *Rajatarangini,* the history of Kashmir is enshrined in three other Sanskrit works of Jonaraja, Srivasa, Prajyabhatta and Suka. Kalhana's Kavya brings down the narrative from traditional history to 1148 A. D., and the other writers who followed him continue the history to the date of the conquest of Kashmir by Akbar, 1588. Prajyabhatta having left his MS. imperfect, it was completed by Suka.

The papers that these volumes comprise are : (i) "An Essay on the Hindu History of Cashmir" by H. H. Wilson, first published in the *Asiatic Researches,* Serampore, Vol. XV, 1825, pp. 1-119, (ii) "Kings of Kashmir" by R. C. Dutt,—*Calcutta Review,* July 1880, and (iii) Buhler's Report of a Tour in search of Sanskrit MSS made in Kashmir, Rajputana and Central India,—*The Indian Antiquary,* September, 1877.

It has not appeared desirable to cumber the text with diacritical marks, but long vowels are marked where necessary as a guide to pronunciation. Consonants may be pronounced as in English. Short *a* with stress is pronounced like *u* in *but,* e. g., *Chandra* is pronounced *Chundrā* ; the short *a* without stress being an abstract vowel like the *A* in *America.* Other vowels are to be pronounced as in Italian ; e. g., *Mir* is pronounced *Meer, Yusuf* is pronounced as *Yoosuf. E* and *o* are long, whether marked or not. *Au* is pronounced as *aw,* as in *Kanauj* or *Kānouj.*

INTRODUCTION

The only Sanskrit composition yet discovered, to which the title of History, can with any propriety be applied is the *Rajatarangini,* a history of Kashmir, This work was first introduced to the knowledge of the Muhammadans by the learned minister of Akbar, Abul Fazl, but the summary which he has given of its contents, was taken as he informs us from a Persian translation of the Hindu original, prepared by order of Akbar. The example set by that liberal monarch, introduced amongst his successors, and the literary men of their reigns, a fashion of remodelling, or retranslating the same work, and continuing the history of the province, to the periods at which they wrote.

The earliest work of this description, after that which was prepared by order of Akbar, is one mentioned by Bernier, who states an abridged translation of the *Rajatarangini* into Persian, to have been made, by command of Jahangir; he adds, that he was engaged upon rendering this into French, but we have never heard anything more of his translation; at a subsequent period, mention is made in a later composition, of two similar works, by Mulla Hussain, Kari, or the reader, and by Hydar Malek, *Chandwaria,*[1] whilst the work, in which this notice occurs, the *Wakiat-i-Kashmir* was written in the time of Mohammed Shah, as was another history of the province, entitled the *Nawadir-ul-Akhbar.* The fashion seems to have continued to a very recent date, as Ghulam Hussain,[2] notices the composition of a history of Kashmir having been entrusted to various learned men, by order of Jivana the Sikh, then Governor of the province, and we shall have occasion to specify one history of as recent a date, as the reign of Shah Alam.

The ill-directed and limited enquiries of the first European settlers in India, were not likely to have traced the original of these Muhammadan compositions, and its existence was little adverted to, until the translation of the *Ayin-i-Akbari* by Francis Gladwin was published (1783-6). The abstract then

[1] A summary taken from this work and which appears to have been the one alluded to by Bernier, is given in the *Description de l' Inde* from Tieffenthaler, vol. I. p. 89

[2] *Seir Mutakherin,* vol. 3, p. 210.

given naturally excited curiosity, and stimulated enquiry, but the result was unsatisfactory, and a long period intervened before the original work was discovered[3] Sir William Jones was unable to meet with it, although the history of India from the Sanskrit-Kashmir authorities, was amongst the tasks his undaunted and indefatigable intellect had planned, and it was not until the year 1805, that H. T. Colebrooke[4] was successful in his search. At that time he procured a copy of the work from the heirs of a Brahman, who died in Calcutta, and about the same time, or shortly afterwards, another transcript of the *Rajatarangini* was obtained by Peter Speke from Lucknow. To these two copies I have been able to add a third, which was brought for sale in Calcutta ; and I have only to add, that both in that city and at Banaras, I have been hitherto unable to meet with any other transcript of this curious work.

The *Rajatarangini* has hitherto been regarded as one entire composition ; it is however in fact a series of compositions, written by different authors, and at different periods ; a circumstance that gives greater value to its contents, as with the exception of the early periods of the history, the several authors may be regarded almost as the chroniclers of their own times. The first of the series is the *Rajatarangini* of Kalhana Pandit, the son of Champaka, who states his having made use of earlier authorities, and gives an interesting enumeration of several which he had employed. The list includes the general works of Suvrata and Narendra ; the History of Gonarda and his three successors, by Hala Raja, an ascetic ; of Lava, and his successors to Asoka, by Padma Mihira ; and of Asoka and the four next princes by Sri Ch'havillachara. He also cites the authority of Nila Muni, meaning probably the *Nila Purana*, a Purana known only in Kashmir ; the whole forming a remarkable proof of the attention bestowed by Kashmirian writers upon the history of their native country : an attention the more extraordinary, from the contrast it affords, to the total want of historical enquiry in any other part of the extensive countries peopled by the Hindus. The history of Kalhana commences with the fabulous ages, and comes down to the reign of Sangrama Deva, the nephew of Didda Rani, in Saka 949, or A.D. 1027, approaching to what appears to have been his own date, Saka 1070 or A.D. 1148.

[3] *Asiatic Researches*, vol. i, p. 431 ; and vol. iv, p. 188.

[4] *Asiatic Researches*, vol. ix, p. 294.

The next work is the *Rajavati* of Jona Raja, of which I regret to state I have not yet been able to meet with a copy. It probably begins where Kalhana stops, and it closes about the time of Zain-ul-Abidin, or the year of the Hijra 815, as we know from the next of the series.

The *Sri Jaina Rajatarangini* is the work of Sri Vara Pandita, the pupil of Jona Raja, whose work it professes to continue, so as to form with it, and the history of Kalhana, a complete record of the kingdom of Kashmir. It begins with Zain-ul-Abidin, whose name the unprepared reader would scarcely recognise, in its Nagari transfiguration, of Sri Jaina Ollabha Dina, and closes with the accession of Fatteh Shah, in the year of the Hijra 882, or A. D. 1477. The name which the author has chosen to give his work of *Jainatarangini* has led to a very mistaken notion of its character; it has been included amongst the productions of Jaina literature, whilst in truth the author is an orthodox worshipper of Siva, and evidently intends the epithet he has adopted as complimentary to the memory of Zain-ul-Abidin, a prince who was a great friend to his Hindu subjects, and a liberal patron of Hindu letters and literary men.

The fourth work, which completes the aggregate current under the name of *Rajatarangini,* was written in the time of Akbar, expressly to continue to the latest date, the productions of the author's predecessors, and to bring the history down to the time at which Kashmir became a province of Akbar's empire. It begins accordingly where Sri Vara ended, or with Fatteh Shah, and closes with Nazek Shah, the historian apparently, and judiciously, avoiding to notice the fate of the kingdom during Humayun's retreat into Persia. The work is called the *Raja vali Pataka,* and is the production of Punya or Prajnya Bhatta.

Of the works thus described, the manuscript of Peter Speke[5] containing the compositions of Kalhana and Sri Vara, came into my possession at the sale of that gentleman's effects. Of Henry Thomas Colebrooke's manuscript, containing also the work of Punya Bhatta, I was permitted by that gentleman, with the liberality I have had former occasion to acknowledge, to have a transcript made; and the third manuscript, containing the same three works, I have already stated I procured by accidental purchase. Neither of the three comprises the work of

[5] Peter Speke (1745-1811), Civil Service, Member of the Supreme Council, died in Calcutta.

Jona Raja, and but one of them, the transcript of Colebrooke's manuscript, has the third *Taranga* or section of Kalhana's history. The three manuscripts are all very inaccurate; so far so indeed, that a close translation of them, if desirable, would be impracticable.[6] The leading points, however, may be depended upon, agreeing not only in the different copies, but with the circumstances narrated in the Compendium of Abul Fazl, and in the Mahammadan or Persian histories which I have been able to procure.

The Persian works which I have consulted are the following: the *Nawadir-ul Akhabar,* the work of Rafiuddin Mohammed, the *Wakiat-i-Kashmir* by Mohammed Azim, the *Tarikh Kashmir* of Narayan Kul, and the *Goheri Alem Tohfet us shahi,* by Badia-ud-din. The first of these authors has the advantage of being a Kashmirian by birth, although descended of a Balkh family. He alludes to the work of Kalhana Pandit, which he avows his purpose of correcting where at variance with the true faith; and it must be acknowledged, that he has altered without remorse, although it may be questioned, whether he has corrected. His chief disagreements are those of omission however, as in the Hindu portion of his history, he occasionally passes over whole dynasties, and connects the *disjuncta membra* of his original, with very little regard to accuracy of time or descent. The date of his work is 1133 of the Hijra, in the reign of Mohammed Shah.

The *Wakiat-i-Kashmir* contains a much fuller account of the province, and is a closer approximation to the Hindu original. The History follows the order of the Sanskrit work very regularly, but the work is not confined to the History of Kashmir, two of the three portions into which it is divided being appropriated to the description of the country, its natural and arti-

[6] Since this was written in 1825, the following among other editions of *Rajatarangini* have seen the light of day: 1. *Rajatarangini: histoire des rois du Kachmir*; tr. et commpar M. A. Troyer, Paris, 1840-52, 3 vols. 2. J. C. Datta: *Kings of Kashmira,* 3. vols., Calcutta, 1879-98. 3. M.A. Stein: *Rajatarangini* or *Chronicle of the Kings of Kashmir,* First Edition, Text. 1892, Do. Eng. Tr 1900. 4. Durga Prasad: *The Rajatarangini of Kalhana* Text only, 1892. 5. *Rajatarangini: The Saga of the Kings of Kashmir. The River of Kings* by R. S. Pandit, 1935. First translation of a portion of the *Rajatarangini* was in Persian made by order of King Zain-ul-Abidin of Kashmir (1421-72 A.C.) who named the version "The Sea of Tales", 1835 (A. S. Ed.).

ficial curiosities, and the religious and literary characters it has given birth to since the establishment of Islam. Mohammed Azim, the author, calls himself the son of Khair-uz-zaman Khan, and writes in the year of the Hijra 1140; living therefore, as well as Rafi-ud-din, in the reign of Mohammed Shah. The same reign produced the third work, which is professedly a translation of the *Rajatarangini*. It has all the usual defects of oriental translation, and follows the original with a whimsical interchange of fidelity and variation; some passages, especially those of a legendary character, being minutely given, whilst others of more historical importance are imperfectly rendered or altogether omitted. The author, Narayan Kul, was a Hindu Brahman and a native of Kashmir.

The last work enumerated is of very modern date, having been written in the time of the last Shah Alam; the author Bedia-ud-Din was the son of Mohammed Azim, the author of the *Wakiat*, whose omissions he purposes to supply, from authorities peculiarly his own, and of which he had subsequently become possessed. He particularly specifies the *Nur Namah*, an ancient history of Kashmir, written by Shaikh Nur-ud-Din Wali in the Kashmirian language and rendered into Persian by Moulavi Ahmed Almeh, in the reign of Zain-ul-Abidin. A copy of this the author had procured from one of the descendants of the last independant princes of Kashmir, who were settled as private individuals in Akbarabad or Agra; and it is to be presumed that to this work Bedia-ud-Din owes the extraordinary additions which he has made occasionally to the labours of his predecessors, and their common original. None of the works above particularised, offer much valuable illustration of the Sanskrit original history; nor do they furnish any additions of historical importance. As well as the summary of Abul Fazl however they are very useful in corroborating or explaining many parts of the Sanskrit text, whilst they do comprise a few additional circumstances, which are curious at least in their origin and character, although very questionable in point of probability or truth. The chief value of these works, however, is the notice they take, of the comparatively modern condition of many towns and temples, the foundation of which is commemorated by the Hindu writers, and the existence of which at all, cannot perhaps now be verified, except upon the testimony of these Muhammadan authors; the short interval that has elapsed since their days, having been sufficient to sweep away the vestiges of of antiquity, which in their time continued to bear witness to the public spirit, and munificence, of the Hindu sovereigns of Kashmir.

In the utter darkness which envelopes the history of India previous to the Muhammadan invasion, the appearance of such a record as that furnished us by the Kashmirian writers acquires an importance, not otherwise derived from the value of the record itself, nor the character of the transactions it commemorates. It being the sole luminary, however, of the gloomy interval alluded to, renders us naturally curious to follow the track it singly serves to light, and the history of Kashmir, has accordingly attracted the attention of those best competent to have prosecuted the investigation. I have already stated it to be one of the desiderata of Sir William Jones; and at the time that Henry Colebrooke announced the discovery of the manuscript, he also declared his intention of giving to the public an account of its contents. The execution of his purpose has probably been impeded by other more important labours, and the too contracted term of Sir William Jones's splendid career, disappointed his hope of performing this, and greater undertakings. A more satisfactory account of the contents of the *Rajatarangini* than that furnished by Abul Fazl is therefore still a desideratum, and in the little probability that now exists of the task being undertaken by living talent more adequate to its accomplishment, I have been induced to prepare, from it chiefly, the following sketch of the Hindu History of Kashmir.

The want of a copy of the connecting series of Jona Raja, and the occupation of the works of Sri Vara and Punya Bhatta by Musalman transactions, will prevent me, at present at least, from extending the limits of my essay, beyond those of Kalhana Pandit, or following any other Hindu guide. His work as a historical composition is clear and consistent, and contains fewer extravagances than most of the works to which the name of history has been assigned by unphilosophical and credulous people. Like the mass of the Hindu compositions on all subjects, it is written in verse, and as a poem it contains many passages of merit, both in sentiment and style. The summary of its contents given by Abul Fazl is too concise to be of much service, and in the transformation of names occasioned by the difficulty of expressing the Nagari alphabet in Persian characters, excites not infrequently a doubt, whether the persons named were possessed of Hindu appellations. Further, it is in many places inaccurate, and it does not therefore preclude a necessity, for some such fuller account of the *Rajatarangini* and its contents, as is attempted in this essay, and which whilst it follows the order and authority of Kalhana Pandit, proposes to comprehend such occasional illustration of his history of Kashmir, as may be derived from the Muhammaden writers above mentioned, or from classical authorities, or more modern investigation.[7]

[7] Jogesh Chunder Dutt, elder brother of Romesh Chunder Dutt, writes as follows in the prefaces to the first and second volumes (1879-98) of his English translation of Kalhana Pandit's *Rajatarangini* :

"The first part of the book was written by Kalhana Pandit, son of Champaka. It embraces the history of the country, from the earliest period to the time of the author, A. D. 1148. The next part entitled Rajabali was written by Jonaraja, and brought the history down to A. D. 1412; and this again has been continued under the name of Jainarajatarangini by his pupil Sri Vora Pandit to A. D. 1477. The fourth and last part, the Rajavalipitaka brings down the history of the country to the time of its conquest by Akbar, and was written by Priya Bhatta at the time of the emperor......"

"Kalhana was contemporaneous with the last king whose account is narrated in his history, and probably he used to read his work, from time to time, at the court of his sovereign. He has consequently made every effort to justify the conduct of the princes of the usurping dynasty, and to censure, often unjustly, the conduct of the last king of the previous line. Writing for a courtly audience, Kalhana often indulges in style which is more artistic than clear, and his love of alliteration has clouded many an important passage. In several places, persons and events have been referred to by him so incidentally as to make it extremely difficult for us to identify them, though the sense was no doubt clear......And, lastly, his narration too is not faultless. Not only does he often attach undue importance to insignificant incidents, but he also travels from subject to subject without having the patience to complete the account of any one of them. He might have left us much more of useful and valuable information of his own times than he has done".

"As regards the history of times anterior to his, all that can be said is, that, in the absence of any other historical records, his must be considered very valuable. Wherever light has been received from other sources, his account appears to be meagre and incomplete, though generally correct".—Ed.

CHAPTER I

The Hindu History of Kashmir commences with the statement, that the beautiful valley forming that kingdom was originally a vast lake, called Satisaras,[1] and this assertion has not only been copied by the Muhammadan writers, but it agrees with the local traditions of the country, and as far as probablity is regarded, has received the sanction of that able geographer James Rennel.[2]

The draining of the water from the valley is ascribed, by the Hindu historians to the Saint Kasyapa, the son of Marichi, the

[1] *Sati*, a virtuous woman, and *Saras*, a lake; the original does not give the etymology, but Abul Fazl makes it the Lake of Uma, the wife of Mahadeva, one of whose names, it is true, is Sati in the character of a virtuous spouse.

Kashmir pesh az imarat Sati Sar nam dasht
Sati nam-i-zan ast wa sar nam-i-hauz-i-Kalan

Wakiat-i-Kashmir. So Abdul Fazl, Gladwin's translation, vol. ii. p. 169. Barnier says, "stories about the ancient kings of Kashmir seem to indicate that the whole country was nothing but a vast lake." And according to Forster, the legends of the country assert that Solomon visited the valley, and finding it covered, except one eminence, with a noxious water, which had no outlet, he opened a passage in the mountains, and gave to Kashmir its beautiful plains.

From the general concurrence of the Persian writers, with the account of the Hindu historians, must be excepted Bedia-ud-din; he begins with the creation, and brings Adam from Sarandip, where all Muhammadan authorities place him after the fall, to Kashmir. The sovereignty of Kashmir continued in the line of Seth for 1110 years, when the Hindus conquered the Province under Harinand Raja, and his family ruled it till the period of the deluge. After the flood Kashmir was peopled by a tribe from Turkestan. The inhabitants were taught the worship of one God, by Moses, who died there, and whose tomb or place of sepulture is still to be seen in Kashmir. The relapse of the Kashmirians into the Hindu idolatry was punished by the local inundation of the province and the solitary supremacy of the Afrit, Jaladeo, as described in the *Wakiat-i-Kashmir*. See Appendix No. 1. These details are sufficient to give an idea of Bedia-ud-din's, or probably of the Shaikh Nur-ud-din's, historical merits.

[2] "So far am I from doubting the tradition respecting the existence of the Lake that covered Kashmir, that appearances alone would serve to convince me without either the tradition or the History." *Memoir of a Map of Hindostan*, 1783, p. 107.

son of Brahma, the Kashef or Kasheb of the Muhammadans, according to some of whom, he was not the Hindu Seer, but a Deo or Genie, the servant of Suliman, by whose orders he effected the desiccation of Kashmir. The method of doing this was opening a passage through the mountain at Baramulah,[3] by which the water passed off; but the Hindu accounts do not specify the channel by which Kasyapa originally drained the valley. As however it is not improbable that the valley was really submerged, it is equally possible, as Bernier supposes,[4] that some natural convulsion rent the confining mountainous barrier, and opened to the waters, an outlet to the plains of the Punjab.

The district thus recovered by Kasyapa, was also it is said peopled by him, with the assistance of the superior deities, whom he brought from heaven for that purpose, at the beginning of the seventh or present *Manwantara.* We must of course subject Kashmir to the same periods of destruction and renovation, as the other parts of the universe, if we wish to reconcile this date with the usual chronology, but as this is not very indispensable, it has been overlooked by the original authority. We also have nothing in the Sanskrit text here, respecting the colony of Brahmins, whom Abul Fazl says, he introduced into the province, and from which it might be inferred that he then introduced the Brahmanical religion, an event that probably occurred, as we shall see, at a subsequent period; the worship in Kashmir, being in the meantime apparently that of the Nagas or snake Gods;[5] a superstition of very obvious occurrence, amongst the rude inhabitants of a country, recently recovered from the waters,

[3] The *Wakiat-i-Kashmir* has another legend relative to the opening on this occasion of the Baramulah pass, which is ascribed to Vishnu; the story is not worth quoting, except as a curious specimen of a Muhammadan disposition to enlarge upon Hindu fable; not a syllable of the legend is to be found in the *Rajatarangini.* See Appendix No. 1.

[4] "For myself, I would not wish to deny that the whole of this land was formerly covered with water. The same thing is said about Thessaly and some other countries. I can hardly believe that this is the work of men, for the mountain is too high and too large. It is my belief that an earth tremor, to which these regions are subject, opened up a subterranean cavern through which the mountain was pushed out." -*Voyage de Kachemire.* The remark made by Bernier continues applicable to the neighbouring and analogous districts: during the labours of Hodgson in Garwhal, in 1817, he noticed forty shocks.

[5] See Appendix No. 2.

and consequently abounding with the venomous reptiles common to slimy and marshy places.[6]

From the period of the first settlement of Kashmir to the reign of Gonarda, the first prince whose name has been recorded, the country was governed by a succession of 52 kings of the Kaurava family, whose reigns formed a period of 1266 years;[7] these princes were not worthy of record, says our Hindu author, on account of their disregard of the precepts of the Vedas, and their impure and vicious lives; and he assigns a better reason for their being forgotten, did they ever indeed exist, in this expression, *kartārāḥ kīrtikāyasya nābhuvankavivedhasaḥ* which we may employ Horace to translate, *Illacrymabiles urgentur ignotique longa nocte, carent quia vate sacro.*

The blank thus left in the history by the Hindu writer, is partly filled up by Muhammadan authortiy, and we may therefore here desert our usual guide to contemplate the series of monarchs, derived from another source. According to Bedia-ud-Din, after the settlement of the country by Suliman, he left the sovereignty to his cousin, Isaun, who reigned over Kashmir twenty-five years and was succeeded by his son.

2. Kassalgham, who fixed his capital at Islamabad and reigned nineteen years. 3. Maherkaz his son succeeded and reigned thirty years. Being childless, he adopted for his son and successor 4. Bandu or Pandu Khan. The birth of this prince was miraculously effected, his mother becoming pregnant from bathing in a reservoir or tank; his death was equally marvellous, as upon bathing himself in the same reservoir, he dissolved and returned to the element whence he sprang. He is said to have

[6] With respect to the Leader of the colony, Hamilton correctly observes, much confusion prevails, arising probably from different persons being designated by the name Kasyapa. He has endeavoured to distinguish three of the names. Ist. "Kasyapa Muni, son of Marichi : 2nd. Kasyapa married to the daughter of Daksha, also named Tarkshya, who led a colony of civilized people into Kashmir. And 3rd. Kasyapa married to the daughters of Vaiswanara, grandson of the preceding."—*Genealogies of the Hindus*. There is reason to fear however that this distinction can scarcely be made out on original authority. Hamilton's chronology would rather confirm the assertion of the text that it was the son of Marichi who colonised Kashmir, for he places this sage in the 20th century before the Christian era, and it appears not unlikely that Kashmir was colonised about that period.

[7] So also the *Ain-i-Akbari* : the author of *Wakiat-i-Kashmir* cities Hindu authority, for a series of 55 Princes and a period of 1919 years.

had a most numerous offspring, and to have seen in his life time, no fewer than fifteen thousand descendants; these were the Pandavas, afterwards so celebrated in Indian History.

We may here pause to notice the concurrence of this account with that which we have already extracted from Hindu authority, of the subjection of Kashmir to a long series of Kaurava princes, as these are in the estimation of the Hindus, the offspring of a common ancestor, and virtually the same with the Pandava race. This position of the family in the north-west of India, is referred to in many works, and the chief scene of their early exploits is the Punjab, and its vicinity; and these traditions therefore although much embarrassed by uncertainty and fiction, seem to support the idea that this part of India was the native seat of the Pandavas. Besides the positive assertions to this effect in the history of Kashmir, I find that in an unfinished manuscript essay by Wilford, and liberally put into my hands by that eminent scholar, he has also particularised Kashmir as the birth-place of the Pandavas upon Hindu authority, and we find in classical authors [8] the realm or city of Panda, or of the Pandavas, in a similar direction, although not precisely the same position. At the same time, it is true, that Kuru the progenitor of the Kaurava and Pandava races is placed by the Pauranic writers in a more central part of India, and made king of Hastinapur; the five suppositious sons of Pandu were however according to the same authorities actually born in the Himalaya mountains, [9]

[8] Appendix No. 3.

[9] *evam Pandoh sutah pancha devadatta mahavalah*
sambhutah kirtimantascha Kuruvamsa-vivardhanah
subhalakshanasampannah Somavat priyadarsanah
simhadarpa mahesvasah simhavikrantagaminah
simhagriva manushyendra vavrdhurdevavikramah
vivardhamanaste tatra pura Himavato girau

Mahabharata. Adi Parva (2. 64.) "Thus the five God-given sons of Pandu grew up in the holy mountain of Himavat, endowed with divine force, with the strength, the gait and prowess of lions, expert archers, lovely as the moon, and graced with every auspicious mark, renowned through the world, and honouring the race of Kuru." In the first or *Anukramanic* portion of the *Mahabharata* a curious passage occurs relative to the spurious descent of the Pandavas, for when the boys are brought to Hastinapur by the Rishis, their preceptors, some of the citizens say, they cannot be the sons of Pandu, for he has long been dead; *yada chiramrtah Pandu katham tasya te chapare*—the passage is not the less remakable from its being singular, that is to say, it is not adverted whither Pandu with his wife Kunti had accompanied the Rishis, and where the Gods descended to rear posterity for the prince; there can be little doubt therefore that either the original Kaurava family, or a very important branch of it, came from the north-west and mountainous parts of India.[10]

To return however to the series of princes enumerated by Bedia-ud-din; we have, 5. Ladi Khan, son of Pandu Khan. 6. Leddar Khan, his son. 7. Sundar Khan in whose reign the idolatry of the Hindu worship again made its appearance; the prince was slain in endeavouring to obstruct its progress, and was succeeded by 8. Kundar Khan his son, who reigned thirty-five years. 9. Sundar Khan, the second. Idolatry was now the national religion, and the king erected a temple to Sadasiva. 10. Tundu Khan 11. Beddu Khan, who reigned 115 years. 12. Mahand Khan. 13. Darbinash Khan. 14. Deosir Khan. 15. Tehab Khan. This prince was attacked and slain by his neighbour and relation, the king of Kabul, who seized upon the throne of Kashmir, and reigned under the name of 16. Kalju Khan; after a reign of seven years he was driven out by his Pandava relatives, who raised to the throne 17. Surkhab Khan; his reign lasted 191 years. 18. Sharmabaram Khan. 19. Naurang Khan; this prince was a great conqueror and extended his dominions to the kingdom of China. 20 Barigh Khan. 21 Gawasheh Khan. 22. Pandu Khan the second; he recovered the provinces that had been subject to the crown of Kashmir, and which extended to the shores of the Indian sea. 23. Haris Khan; his reign lasted 23 years. 24. Sanzil Khan. 25. Akbar Khan. 26. Jabar Khan. 27. Naudar Khan: he introduced the worship of fire. 28. Sankar Khan, who was attacked and slain by Bakra Raj, a neighbouring chief who headed the Kashmirian nobles driven into rebellion by the tyranny of their king.

to in the subsequent part of the poem which details the event at length. The *Anukramanika* is a summary of the whole work, and not impossibly the original, the bulk of the poem being merely a repitition and expansion of the brief narration, which it contains.

[10] As one additional argument, the complexion of Pandu may be mentioned; it is said in the *Mahabharata* that he was named Pandu, pale, from the paleness of his colour. Vyasa says to the younger widow of his late brother:

> *yasmatpandutvamapanna virupam prekshya mamiha*
> *tasmadeva sutastavai pandureva bhavishyati*
> *namachasyaitadeveha bhavishyati subhanane*
>
> *Mahabharata.* Adi Parva.

The six sons of Sankar Khan succeeded in due order to their father's sovereignty, and also to his fate. Their accession and deaths were the work of a few hours, whence originated the proverb, said to be still current in Kashmir: *Yak deg t'ām bar digarān tā hangām-i- ukhtan haft bādshāhī dīd*

"One caldron, on one fire, saw seven kings before the flesh was boiled," a proverb, which though not of literal, has been in a general sense of not inappropriate application, to events of eastern history, of a more authentic character, than the one to which its origin is here ascribed.

29. Bakra Raj then took possession of Kashmir, and bequeathed it to his descendants; their names are however unknown, and a blank interval precedes the succession of Augnand the first monarch, with whom all the authorities are agreed to commence, what may be regarded, as the dawn of legitimate historical record.

The list above inserted, although of an obviously fabulous construction, still contains matter to excite curiosity, and awaken some speculation as to the possibility of any part of it being true; it seems very probable that it originates with tradition, and is not altogether unfounded, although no doubt much disfigured, and most probably misplaced; the title of Khan attached to the names, few of which too appear to be Hindu, indicates a race of Tartar princes, and we shall have occasion to notice the presence of Tartar rulers in Kashmir, accompanied with something like chasms in the history, which Bedia-ud-Din's catalogue would enable us to fill, conveniently enough; if we might conjecture from the names of several princes on the west of India, the invasion of Alexander was the period of Tartar rule in this direction, as Oxycanus and Musicanus might easily be resolved into Tartar appellations with the designation Khan attached;[11] it may be resting too much on conjecture only, however, to give

[11] I am not disposed to attach any importance to etymological conjectures in general, and merely adduce such analogies, as possible identifications in the absence of better guides; at the same time I am very much disposed to think with Vincent, that "most if not all of the Indian names, which occur in classical authors, are capable of being traced to native appellations, existing at this day among the Hindoos, at least, if not the Moguls." (*Voyage of Nearchus*, 129). Pottinger finds a similarity between Musicanus and Moo-Sehwan, the names of two contiguous districts in Sind, and usually connected in utterance. They lie exactly, where we are told, the Greeks found that chief's territories.—*Travels in Biloochistan.*

a period of existence to what are perhaps after all but phantoms, and we must remain satisfied with the possibility, that they were real personages, who ruled Kashmir as foreigners, and that as foreigners, they were extruded from the Hindu annals, and were preserved only by undefined traditions, which have been embodied into the Muhammadan history of Shaikh Nuruddin with little regard to chronology, or truth.

As the first named sovereign of the Hindu history of Kashmir, succeeded to the princes who had governed the country for nearly thirteen centuries, there should have been little or no chronological difficulty about the period of his accession; the introduction of *Manwantaras* and *Kalpas*, has however obscured a system, otherwise clear at least, if not unexceptionable, and has left it doubtful, whether these princes, as well as the first settlement of the country, come within the limits of the Kali-age, and consequently at what date in that age, Gonarda, the Augnand,[12] of the Muhammadan writers, was king of Kashmir. There are other chronological points, connected with his history, that have received the notice of the Hindu historian.

The passage of the original is however here not very distinct and refers evidently to computations of an uncommon character. Gonarda as appears from the transactions of his reign, was contemporary with Krishna and Yudhisthir, who according to the generally received notions, lived at the end of the Dwapara age; this however the author observes is irreconcilable with the series of Gonarda's successors, which agrees better with the opinion, that places the existence of the Kaurava and Pandava princes about the middle of the seventh century of the Kali Yuga (age), a computation it may be remarked which is at variance with Gonarda's succeeding to the throne, after that had been occupied for 1266 years, unless some of those years be carried into the preceding age; it is of very little use however to attempt to reconcile these discrepancies, as the different statements are all probably equally incorrect; and it is only of importance to observe the disagreement between this author and the popular belief as to the age of Yudhisthir and Krishna, and the reduction of the antiquity usually assigned to them, which is thus

[12] In Nagari *gonarda* or in some copies *gonanda*. the Persian is *augand* and the author of the *Wakiat-i-Kashmir* as well as Bedia-ud-Din leave no doubt of the intention of the Musalman writers as they detail the letters of this and other names, in the manner, common in Arabic and Persian Lexicons.

derivable from Hindu authority; any other conclusions we shall be better prepared to make when we have gone through the different dynasties of princes, and the events recorded to have happened during their reigns.[13] If we may trust the Hindu historian, Gonarda the First was a relation of Jarasandha, king of Magadha, to whose assistance he led an army from Kashmir. The confederates were opposed to Krishna, in the province of Mathura, and were defeated in an engagement upon the banks of Jamuna by the chief, and his brother Balarama, by whose hands Gonarda was slain, whilst attempting to rally his flying troops.[14] The prince was succeeded by his son Damodara who in his impatience to revenge his father's death, attacked a party of the friends of Krishna on their return from a marriage in Gandhara on the Indus;[15] the bride was killed in the affray; but the rage of the bridegroom and his friends was irresistible, and the followers of the prince were defeated, and himself slain; the whole transaction being such as was probably of not infrequent occurrence, in the history of these mountainous regions, in a state of society much more advanced, than that of which it is narrated. Damodara left his wife Yasovati pregnant, and ill able to resist the victorious Yadava. Krishna however sent Brahmans to appease her anxiety, and establish her in the kingdom, silencing the remonstrances of his friends by this quotation from the Puranas:

Kāśmīrāḥ pārvatī tatra rājā jñeyo Harāṃśajaḥ
nāvajñeyaḥ sa dushṭo'pi vidushā bhūtimichchhatā

"Kashmir is as Parvati,[16] and the king is a portion of Hara; if even vicious therefore, he is not to be disrespected by the sage who hopes for heaven."

In due time Yasovati was delivered of a son, who was immediately anointed king,[17] the minister of his father conducting the affairs of the state during his minority; he was named

[13] Appendix 4.
[14] Appendix 5.
[15] Appendix 6.

[16] This appears to be a pun, Parvati meaning both mountinous and the wife of Siva.

[17] There is no other word that can be used to express the *Abhishek* considered an essential part of the ceremony of coronation; the word means in fact sprinkling, and implies in these cases, the sprinkling of the king with water from some sacred stream, as the Ganges, &c.

Gonarda[18] after his grand-father; his tender years prevented him from taking any part in the war that continued during his youth, to rage between the Kaurava and Pandava families.

A dark period follows the reign of this prince, and the chasm is filled by a nameless troop of thirty-five kings, who deviating from the precepts of the Vedas were consequently immersed in the waters of oblivion;[19] to them succeeded a monarch of some celebrity, Lava, the Loo or Looloo of the Muhammadan historians, of whom the only action recorded is the foundation of the city Lolora,[20] a city which, according to the extravagant accounts of all parties, contained originally an incredible number of stone edifices,[21] and which in modern times, continued to be a celebrated and populous *Tappa* or Village. Lava is also said to have been a benefactor of the Brahmanical tribe.

Kusesaya,[22] the son of Lava, succeeded his father, whom he resembled in conferring endowments of land upon the Brahmanical priesthood.[23] He was followed in habits and sovereignty by his son Khagendra,[24] of whom it is recorded that he constructed the towns Khagi and Ehanmusha.[25] Surendra,[26] the son of this prince succeeded him, and was actively employed in founding towns and building temples and palaces; one city of his construction was Suraka situated near the Darada country, or at the foot the mountains.

According to the Muhammadan writers, this prince had a daughter named Satapan Bhanu of great beauty and accomplishments; the reputation of which induced Bahman, the son of Isfendiar, who afterwards governed Persia under the name of

[18] Abul Fazl has Bala; the designation of the infant monarch, or Bala, a child, having been mistaken for his own appellation.

[19] According to Bedia-ud-din they were all of the Pandava race.

[20] Perhaps the Durroo or Lurroo of Forster, ii. 5.

[21] Abul Fazl has 80 crore; the original, one crore minus 16 lakhs or 84.00,000; both Rafiuddin and Mahommed Azim say, that Looloo or Lolot was a populous place in the Pargana of Kamraj, or the western divisions of Kashmir.—*Ain-i-Akbari*, ii. 162.

[22] Kishn.—Abul Fazl &c.

[23] The term used on these occasions is Agrahara, which imports a portion of land or a village, given to the Brahmans, with or without a temple or dwelling.

[24] Khagunder.—Abul Fazl.

[25] Kakapur and Gowmoha in the time of Muhammadan writers.

[26] Serendair.—Abul Fazl.

Ardisheer Dirazdest, to solicit and obtain the princess in marriage. It does not appear from what source they have derived this story, as it is not found in the Hindu records, nor in the historical romance of Firdausi, unless we suppose it to have originated in the adventures of Gushtasp, the grand father of Bahman, who whilst in exile in the west married Kattyoon, the daughter of the Emperor of Room. (Malcolm's *Persia*, p. 56). Had there been any foundation for the tradition, it might have been of some chronological utility, but it is probably either an idle invention, or it is a misrepresentation of the fables which relate to the adventures of Bahram Ghor, who according to Firdausi, visited India and there married Sipanud the daughter of Shankal king of Kanouj.[27]

As Surendra however had no son, he was succeeded by a prince of another family named Godhara;[28] whose successors, Suvarna, Janaka and Sachinara[29] followed him in regular descent, and continued to build cities, and construct and endow temples for the advantage of the Brahmans, and chiefly it would seem for the worship of Siva. Janaka the second of these princes is said by Bedia-ud-din to have sent one of his sons into Persia, with a hostile force during the reign of Homai ; the invader however was repelled and slain by the Persians under Darab, the son of Bahman.

The last of these princes being childless, the crown of Kashmir reverted to the family of its former rulers, and devolved on

[27] Or rather of the whole tract of country from Kanouj to Khorasan, according to the Persian poet. Thus Bahram, he says, sends an embassy to Shankal, who is sovereign of India from the river of Kanouj to the borders of Sind *binazdik-i-shankal nigahdar-i-hind zi daryai qanauj tamar zi Sind ;* the king in his reply tells him that the region he rules is full of mountains and streams, and extends from Kanouj to Iran in one direction and in the other from Siclab (Sclavonia or Tartary) to China. *bahar-i-bum ra Kuh wa daryast rah niyabad bar in khak bar deukh wa zan ruyi saqlab ta marz chin zi Qanauj ta marz iran zamin*

The Shankal here mentioned is probably the Shinkal of Mirkhond and Ferishta ; they have however added to his history and have made him contemporary with Afrasiab. The union noticed in the text terminated according to Bedia-ud-din unhappily, and Bahman was murdered by the attendants of the princess at her instigation, in resentment of his contemptuous mention of her father ; and he did not perish, he observes, as said by other reports, of the bite of a snake.

[28] Gowdher—*Ain-i-Akbari.*

[29] Suren, Janak and Seijunar—*Ibid.*

Asoka who was descended from the paternal great uncle of Khagendra. This prince, it is said in the *Ain-i-Akbari,* abolished the Brahmanical rites, and subsituted those of Jaina ; from the original however it appears, that he by no means attempted the former of these heinous acts, and that on the contrary, he was a pious worshipper of Siva, an ancient temple of whom in the character of Vijayesa,[30] he repaired. With respect to the second charge there is better foundation for it, although it appears that this prince did not introduce, but invented or originated the Jaina Sasana.[31] He is said to have founded a city called Srinagar, a different place however from the present capital, which is attributed to a much later monarch.[32] In the reign of Asoka, Kashmir was overrun by the *Mlechhas,* for whose expulsion the king obtained from Siva a pious and valiant son, as a reward for the austerities he had practised.[33]

[30] There are a Vijayesa and Vijaya Kshetra at Banaras. The Vijaya Linga adjourned, or in other words, his worship was brought, according to the Kasi Chand from Kashmir. Sec. 69.

Kasmiradiha sampraptam lingam Vijayasamjnitam
sada vijayadam pumsam prachyamsalakatam katat

[31] Bedia-ud-din says, the new faith was brought from Ajem, in which case it must have been the worship of fire that was introduced, a circumstance of no unlikely occurrence, but which at this period of our history is utterly irreconcilable with the chronology of the original, as if it took place after Darab the son of Homai—it very little preceeded Alexander's invasion of India—but we have not yet come to the second Gonarda, who lived, agreeably to the assertion of Kalhana Pandit, 1182 B.C. It must not be forgotten that these Persian transactions are taken from the Muhammadan writers, and are not hinted at in the *Rajatarangini.*

[32] Rafi-ud-Din calls it Babara ; the *Wakiat-i-Kashmir* and Narayan Kul call it *Sir,* and the latter states that it was in Miraj, or the eastern division of Kashmir, and that traces of its site were visible in his time.

[33] The faith of Asoka is a matter of very little moment, as the prince himself is possibly an ideal personage ; as however the comparative antiquity of the Buddhist and Brahmanical creeds in Kashmir has been supposed to be affected by it, and the events subsequently recorded, it may be advisable to give the passages of the original, which show that Asoka was a worshipper of Siva ; it is not improbable however, if we are to attach credit to any part of this portion of the Kashmirian history, that he permittted heretical, possibly Buddhist doctrines, to be introduced into the kingdom during his reign from his Tartar neighbours.

athavahad Asokakhyassatyasandho vasundharam
yah santavrjino raja prapanno jinasasanam

"Then the prince Asoka, the lover of truth, obtained the earth ; who

Jaloka, the son and successor of Asoka, was a prince of great prowess; he overcame the assertors of the Buddhist heresies, and quickly expelled the *Mlechhas* from the country, thence named Ujjhita dimba; he then carried his victorious arms to foreign regions, and amongst others to the North of Persia, which he subjugated in the reign of Darab[34] and then proceeding in an opposite direction he subdued the country of Kanouj.

The conquest of Kanyakubja by this prince is connected with an event not improbable in itself, and which possibly marks the introduction of the Brahmanical creed, in its more perfect form, into this kingdom. Jaloka is said to have adopted thence the distinction of castes, and the practices which were at that time established in the neighbouring districts; he also introduced into the Government the forms and offices elsewhere prevalent, and first assigned titles and duties to the following seven officers of state, the *Dharmadhyaksha*, the justiciary, or chancellor; *Dhana-adhyaksha*, treasurer; *Kosha-adhyaksha*, master of the military stores; *Chamupati*, commander-in-chief; *Duta*, messenger or ambassador; *Purodha*, the royal chaplain or almoner, and the *Daivajnya* or chief astrologer. The eighteen officers, and their duties, were also defined by this prince, who appears to have been the first of the Kashmir kings who introduced religion and government into that kingdom. He is said to have particularly worshipped Siva as Nandesa in consequence of having had read to him the *Nandipurana* by one of Vyasa's scholars; he also

sinning in subdued affections, produced the Jaina Sasana.". This may mean possibly something very different from the received idea, and may imply his neglect of affairs of state through excess of devotion, and his consequently omitting to prevent the intrusion of a foreign power, rather than a foreign faith, into the kingdom, the expulsion of which was the object of his son's birth.

mlechchhaih samchhadite dese sa taduchchhittaye nrpah
tapah samtoshitallebhe Bhutesat sukrtisutam

"The country being overspread with *Mlechhas*, the king for their expulsion obtained from Bhutesa (Siva as the Lord of the elements) pleased with his *Tapas*, an excellent son."—Buchanan has made a strange misquotation from Abul Fazl; (*Asiatic Researches*, vol. vi. p. 165). He calls Asoka Raja Jannat, and says he established in his reign the Brahmanic rites, instead of abolished them as it occurs in the *Ain-i-Akbari*; an error which justly drew down the angry censures of the Oriental Critics in the *Edinburgh Review* for October, 1802, and the *Asiatic Annual Register* of the same year; the *Mlechhas* might have been Scythians or Tartars. See the observations on the Tartar princes.

[34] Bedia-ud-din

erected temples to the same deity as Jyeshta Rudra. This prince was possessed of supernatural powers, and several marvellous stories are narrated of him, which we need not pause to extract; he was also a prince of a generous disposition, and a rigid observer of his word: although devoted to Siva, he forbore in the latter part of his reign from molesting the followers of the Buddhist schism, and even bestowed on them some endowments as the Vihara[35] called Krityasrama in honour of their female divinities, or spirits named Krityadevi, by whom he had been addressed as a Bodhisatva himself.[36] After a long and glorious reign, he went on a pilgrimage to Chiramochana

[35] Vihara is a common Sanskrit word usually employed to designate a Buddhist temple as well as an establishment or college of Buddhist priests. It seems to have been also used by the old Persians in a similar sense, and to have been applied to their fire temples. See Ouseley's *Persia,* p. 126 and note. In the work before us, it has frequently an extended meaning and also signifies a Royal pleasure house or garden.

[36] The divinity who appeared to the prince to intercede for the Buddhists explains the term *Bodhisatwa* :

Bodhisattvaikasaranah kamkshamtyastamasah kshayam
loke bhagavato Lokanathadarabhya kechana
ye jantava gataklesan Bodhisatvavaveditan
sagase'pi na kupyanti kshamaya chopakurvate
bodhim svasyaivayeshyanti te visvadharanodyatah

"Those who are *Bodhisatwas* trusting to the one great refuge, are desirous of the destruction of darkness : they proceed in the universe of the Lord, from the Lord of the universe, and are not wroth sinfully at the distresses inflicted on animal nature unpervaded by waking truth, but alleviate them by patience. Those who seek to understand themselves, they are strenuous in bearing all." A Bodhisatwa is therefore nothing but a man of patience and piety, and may be regarded as a living type and figuratively as a lineal descendant of Buddha; his origin from the Lord of the universe (Lokanath, an epithet of Buddha) in this passage, may be so intended; at the same time it appears that Bodhisatwa is sometimes considered literally as the son of Buddha; *On verra dans la suite de cet ouvrage que Phou-sa ou Boudhisatoua, les fils de Bouddha,* &c.—Remusat, on the polyglot Chinese vocabulary. *Mines de l'orient, vol. iv.* 198 note. The continuation he refers to has not yet been received. The term, as a generic appellation of a living Buddha, is common in all Buddhist countries; one of the Bourkhans of the Calmucks is named Khomschin *Bodi-Sada* (*Pallas. Fr. Trans.* Oct. ii. 222). An Indian teacher of Buddhism who was invited into Tibet, is named Pothi Satho (Giorgi. 240) and according to Loubere one of the names of Sommono Codom (Samana Gotama) amongst the Siamese, is Pouti Sat, or Seigneur Pouti. (*Vie de Thevetat.*)

Tirtha, where after worshipping Jyeshta Rudra, the prince and his queen were both identified with that deity.

The successor of this celebrated monarch was Damodara, of whose descent various opinions were entertained; some deducing him from Asoka and others considering him as sprung from a different family; he was a devout worshipper of Siva; this prince constructed several stone bridges and causeways, the remains of which were visible in modern times; and there were also two remarkable places, which in the time of Mohammed Azim were connected with the legendary history of this prince; the one a set of small irregular springs, and the other a spot of uneven and marshy ground near the city.

On one occasion as Damodara was proceeding to perform his customary ablutions in the Vitasta, he was importuned for food by some hungry Brahmans ; he deferred complying with their solicitations till he had bathed in the river, at some distance ; to shorten the interval they proposed to bring the river to him, and immediately the water of the Vitasta bubbled up from different places near them, forming the springs that are still to be seen; the king was unmoved by this miracle, and being still determined to bathe in the genuine stream, the Brahmans denounced a curse upon him, and transformed him into a snake, in which shape he haunts the ground near the capital, and is often to be seen ; this spot is called Damodar-uder according to Muhammadan accounts.[37]

Damodara was succeeded by three princes who divided the country, and severally founded capital cities named after themselves. These princes were called Hushka, Jushka, and Kanishka,[38] and these appellations are strongly corroborative of an assertion of our author, that they were of Turushka, that is, of Turk or Tartar extraction; they are considered as synchronous, but may possibly be all that are preserved of some series of Tartar princes, who, it is very likely, at various periods, established themselves in Kashmir. The chief event recorded of their reign is the foundation of the three several capitals, named after themselves,[39] but another and more important consequence of their

[37] I understand from some natives of Kashmir that this superstition still exists, and that Damodara, transformed to a serpent, still haunts a lake about seven *cos* from the capital, and is still occasionally visible ; no doubt, in that form.

[38] Beyshek, Reshek, Kinshek.—Abul Fazl. Brothers according to the same authority, but not so termed in the original.

[39] Hushkapur, said by the modern writers to be the modern Sheeroh

sovereignty is said to have been the almost entire change of the national faith, and the nearly exclusive prevalence of the doctrines of the Buddhists under a Bodhisatva or hierarch named Nagarjuna. The period at which this took place is said to have been 150 years before the death of Sakayasinha.[40] The presence of the Turushka princes in Kashmir, we may observe, is in harmony with Tartar traditions; according to these, Oghuz their patriarch is represented to have subdued that country, and introduced the religion of Japhet there, so long back as 2800 years before the Christian era.[41] A second Scythian irruption and subjugation of India, bordering on the Sind is also said to have occurred about the middle of the 7th century before Christ;[42] neither of these dates will correspond precisely with that of the reigns above described, but they are all perhaps equally of little value, and only corroborate the general fact that at some remote period the Tartars or Scythians did govern Kashmir, and render it probable, that they first gave the sanction of authority to their national religion, or that of Buddha, in India.

The Tartar princes were succeeded by Abhimanyu, a monarch evidently of a Hindu appellation, and a follower of the orthodox faith, which he re-established in Kashmir. The chief instrument in this reform was Chandra, a Brahmin celerbated as the author of a grammar, and a teacher of the *Mahabhashya.*[43]

in the Pergannah of Lar, and a town of some extent; Jushkapur and Kanishkapur are identified with Dabimpur and Kansapur, two inconsiderable villages in the time of Mohammed Shah.

[40] Appendix, No. VII.

[41] Oghuz thus conquered the whole of Bokhara, Balkh, Khor, Kabul, Ghazni and Kashmir where there was a very powerful prince named Jagma. *Des Guignes* Tome prem. Partie seconde. p. 10. We cannot find in the text any name resembling the Jagma of the Tartar tradition. but it is apparently a Hindu appellative, and the omission of its original is easily accounted for; we have an evident chasm in the history here, and the accession or expulsion of the Turushka princes is equally unexplained.

[42] Maurice's *Ancient History of India,* Vol ii. p. 224; according to Blair, B. C. 624 in the reign of Cyaxares or Kaikaoos. A subsequent irruption took place in the reign of Darius Hystaspes, if he be, as he probably is, the same with Gushtasp; this last was of a decidedly religious character.—Malcom's *Persia,* vol. i. p. 62.

[43] The name of Chandra occurs amongst the eight ancient Grammarians of the Hindus. Colebrooke on the Sanskrit and Prakrit Languages, *Asiatic Researches,* Vol vii. pp. 204 and 5.

In consequence of the disuse of the prescribed institutes, the abolition of every form of sacrifice, and a departure from the lessons of *Nila Purana,*[44] the Nágas were particularly incensed, and visited the offences of the people with severe and unseasonable storms of rain and snow, in which those especially perished who had adopted the Buddhist heresy ;[45] in this situation of the kingdom, Chandra, descended it is said from Kasyapa, addressed his prayers to Maheswara as Nila Naga, the tutelary deity of the country, and obtained from him a termination of what our author calls, the double plague of Kashmir, the severity of the seasons, and the predominance of the Buddhists.

The reign of Abhimanyu closes the first series of princes, and introduces us to a period in which the author of *Rajatarangini* affects greater precision than before, and specifies the term of each prince's reign; it is evident however that the reigns of the earliest sovereigns are much too protracted, and they must be considerably reduced to be brought within the limits of probability ; the object of the author is evidently to reconcile the details with the gross amount of years, which he has stated to extend, from the first prince of the new series, the third Gonarda, to 1070 of Saka, and which he has made 2330; how far this postulate is correct we are not yet prepared to determine; and must refer its discussion to the close of the history, when we shall have the whole subject before us ; in the meantime the chronology of our author may be admitted, and the dates of the various reigns assigned to them on the principles of his computation; commencing accordingly with the year before Christ 1182 corresponding with 2330 years before Saka 1070 or A.D. 1148.

Gonarda,[46] the third, succeeded Abhimanyu, and prosecuted the reform which that prince had commenced; the ancient ritual agreeably to the Nila precepts, was restored, and the worship of the Nagas and offering of sacrifices re-established ; by acts of this description, the fame of monarchs is perpetuated and this prince gave the same lustre to his family, as Raghava diffused upon the race of Raghu. He reigned 35 years. Gonarda was succeeded by several princes of whom we have only recorded

[44] The Purana of the Naga or Serpent God, named Nila.

[45] Appendix, No. VIII.

[46] According to Bedia-ud-din he was not born but elevated to the throne ; how, is not mentioned ; the same authority makes him subdue, by means of his general Nand Ram, the whole of Hindustan as far as the Narmada.

the dry list of names and the duration of their reigns. These were Vibhishana, who reigned 53 years; Indrajita, 35 years and 6 months; Ravana, 30 years, Vibhishana the second, 35 years and 6 months; making an aggregate of 154 years. Of Ravana, it is said that he extended the worship of Siva as the Linga Vateswara, and of the second Vibhishana that he was both a patron and cultivator of the art of music; the Muhammadan writers say, that in their days Tiranahs ascribed to this prince were current in Kashmir.[47]

B. C. 993 or 490. Nara[48] the son of Vibhishana succeeded his father; this prince began his reign virtuously, but one of his wives having been seduced from her fidelity by a Buddhist ascetic, the king committed a thousand Viharas to the flames, and gave the lands attached to them to the Brahmans; the only measure which seems to authorise the account of Abul Fazl, that in this reign the Brahmans got the better of the followers of Buddha, and burnt down their temples; in fact, however this prince seems to have been as little disposed to regard one sect as the other with complacency, and finally fell a victim, it is said, to the resentment of one of the orthodox priesthood.

The legend which introduces this catastrophe is not without poetical merit, although too purely poetical to be here transcribed at length. A Brahman had become the son-in-law of Susravas, the Naga, whose palace was in a lake, near the borders of the Vitasta, and in a city founded by Nara near that river. The wife of the Brahman, Chandrabaha, residing there with her husband, attracted the illicit affection of the King, and having resisted all his solicitations, obliged him at length to attempt to carry her off by force; the attempt failed ; the Brahman invoked the aid of his father-in-law, who rising from the lake in wrath, excited a violent storm which destroyed the guilty monarch and his people. The sister of the snake God aided him in his attack upon the city with a shower of large stones brought from the Ramanya mountain, the cavities whence they were taken are still, says our author, to be seen. The Nága, a little ashamed of his cruelty, deserted the country, taking with him his son-in-law and his daughter; the waters of the lake he formerly inhabited, he changed to the whiteness of milk, as may be seen at the Amares-

[47] Bedia-ud-din here inserts another prince Indarayan, who was a magician and tyrant, and therefore put to death by his brother Kailas Singh.

[48] Written *Booz* by the Muhammadan writers.

wara Yatra; this lake is sometimes called Jamatrisar; the story is recalled to the minds of men, when they visit Upachakra Dhara.[49] We may observe however that the destruction of the city, and death of this prince, are ascribed by Bedia-ud-din to a popular tumult, excited by the conduct which is here stated to have produced the catastrophe.

Nara was succeeded by his son Siddha, who had escaped the late calamity by having been sent with his nurse to Vijayakshetra some time before. He collected the dispersed and frightened people, and restored prosperity to the kingdom; he reigned sixty years.

We have again a barren series of successive princes, whose names and reigns alone are recorded: Utpalaksha, who reigned 30 years and 6 months; Hiranyaksha, 37 years, 7 months; Hiranyakula, 60 years and Vamakula, 60 years.

B.C. 705 or 310. The last of these was succeeded by his son Mihira Kula,[50] a prince of violent and cruel propensities; the kingdom upon his accession was crowded with *Mlechhas*, although whether as attached to the king, or as enemies, does not appear. The violent disposition of this monarch led him to an attack upon Lanka. The cloth of Sinhala was stamped

[49] Chakder near Mabrah, according to the author of the *Wakiat-i-Kashmir*; Narayana Kul says, there are two fountains, one of the snake and the other of his son-in-law, on the borders of Dutchenpara, and their united water runs to Laider. Abul Fazl speaks of a rivulet with a bed of white clay in this situation (*Ain-i-Akbari*, ii. 133). The origin of this and similar fables is very obvious; they are invented to account for the various phenomena, especially with regard to lakes and springs, with which Kashmir so plentifully abounds. Abul Fazl has a long list of the Ajaibwa Gharaib of this district, and is far from having exhausted the subject, if we may depend upon other authorities. We know less of Kashmir from European enquiry than of almost any other district in the East; it would no doubt amply reward more minute investigation.

[50] These names are strangely transformed in the *Ain-i-Akbari* to Aduthulabch, Hernya, Herenkul, Ebeshek, and Mirkhul. The first prince appears to be intended by the name of Puschcaracsha, which means the same thing, 'the lotus eyed,' who is mentioned in the *Mudra Rakshasa*, as the king of Kashmir, who was one of the princes confederated against Chandragupta or Sandrocottus. The second of the series Hiranyaksha is the hero of a marvellous story in the *Vrihat Katha*, which leads to his marriage with a Vidhyadhari, a Hindu goddess of an inferior order. The prince is called in the *Vrihat Katha*, the son of Kanac'ha; in othere respects there is no question of the identity.

with a golden foot as the seal of its prince; the wife of Mihirakula wearing a jacket of Sinhala cloth, the impression of the seal came off upon her bosom, and the king happening to observe it, was filled with unappeasable indignation, at the idea of the foot of a stranger being impressed upon the bosom of his wife. To revenge the fancied insult, he led his army to Lanka, deposed the King, and placed another on the throne, stipulating that the Sinhala cloths called Yamushadeva should in future bear his own seal, a golden sun. On his way back to Kashmir, he subdued the sovereigns of Chola, Karnata, Lata and other monarchs of the Dakshin. Arrived in Kashmir, he founded the temple of Mihireswara in the capital, and built the city Mihirapur in the district of Holora, in which the Gandhar[51] Brahmans, a low race, and therefore the more highly esteemed by this iniquitous manarch, were permitted to seize upon the endowments of the more respectable orders of the priesthood. According to Mahommed Azim, he also constructed in the pargana of Ouder the Chandrakul canal, which existed in that writer's time.

Two instances of this monarch's ferocious disposition are recorded by the original authority, and have both been transcribed with some alteration by Abdul Fazl and the other Muhammadan authors; on the return of Mihirakula to his own kingdom, one of his elephants fell, whilst proceeding along a narrow defile, and was crushed to pieces by the fall ; the cries of the dying animal were music to the ears of the prince, and so delighted was he with the sound, that he ordered 100 elephants to be precipitated in a similar manner, that his entertainment might be protracted; according to Abdul Fazl the pass was thence called Hasti Wuttar; *Hasti* signifying an elephant and *Wuttar* meaning injury; the latter part of which etymology is scarcely of Sanskrit origin; besides which, that author is a little at variance with himself, as he had previously separated the two words, and told us that they were different portions of the Bember road, through both of which an army might pass. The other anecdote has been supposed to account for the title by which this prince was known of Trikotiha, the slayer of three millions ; amongst the ruins of Narapur, destroyed as we have seen in the reign of Nara by the Naga Susravas, some Khasa tribes had taken up their abode ; to drive them from the prohibited residence, a large stone fell into the bed of the Chandrakula river, and completely obstructed

[51] The *Mahabharata* mentions the Brahmans of this country as of an inferior tribe, as is noticed in Appendix, VI.

the current; the prince was instructed in a dream that its removal could only be effected by a female of unsullied virtue, and he accordingly commanded women of respectable birth and station, to perform the task; their efforts were unavailing; women of the first families and supposed irreproachable conduct, attempted in vain to remove the stone, and its removal was at last effected by a female of a low class, the wife of a potter; the king incensed by this divine proof of the corrupt lives of the female part of his subjects, ordered them to be put to death, together with their husbands, children, and brothers, as implicated in their disgrace.[52] The blood shed by the commands of this sanguinary sovereign was expiated by his death; suffering under a painful disease and awakened to some of his past cruelty, he determined to put a voluntary term to his existence and end his days upon the funeral pile. He found it impossible, however, to meet with persons qualified to conduct the ceremonies of his cremation, as his kingdom was crowded with the impure tribes of Daradas,[53] Bhotiyas and *Mlechhas.* Revoking therefore his grants to the Gandhara Brahmans, he invited those of Aryadesa, on whom he bestowed a thousand Agraharas in Vijayeswara. The pile was constructed of military weapons, and the king having seated himself on the summit, the fire was applied and quickly put a period to his sufferings and his crimes. The duration of his reign is said to have been 70 years.

Vaka,[54] the son of Mihira Kula succeeded his father; he founded the city Lavanotsa on the banks of Vakavati river ; he was prevailed upon to assist a Yogiswari at a rite, which enabled her to traverse the air at a spot where the impression of her knees is still visible on a rock.[55] He was accompanied by a hundred of his descendants, and the legand of Satakapalesa and the Matrichakra stone is still commemorated at Khira Matha or Khira College. Vaka reigned 63 years and 13 days. The names and reigns of his immediate successors are all that has been recorded of them :

[52] The point of this story is the same as of that related of Pheron by Herodotus, vol. ii. p. 111 and *Ancient Universal History* Vol. i. p. 294.

[53] *Asiatic Researches,* vol. vi. p. 417. Daward, the mountainous range north west of Kashmir, and the present residence of the Durds.

[54] Beck.—*Ain-i-Akbari.*

[55] At Beren or Meren according to Narayan Kul, who adds that she killed the king ; the subsequent allusion is not further explained by Kalhana Pandit.

Kshitinanda, ruled 30 years; Vasunanda, 52 years and 2 months; Bara, 60 years; and Aksha,[56] 60 years.

B. C. 370 or 130. A Kama Sastra is ascribed to the second of these princes. Aksha was succeeded by his son Gopaditya,[57] a prince of eminent piety, whose virtue brought back the *Satya Yuga* or golden age; he enforced a strict observance of the ritual and distinctions of caste, removed those Brahmans who had adopted impure practices from their endowments, and invited others from distant countries to replace them, and finally he forbade the killing of any animal except for the purpose of sacrifice. According to the Muhammadan authorities, he built a temple, or the mound near the capital of Kashmir, called the Takht Suliman;[58] it was destroyed with other places of Hindu worship by Sekandar,[59] one of the first Muhammadan kings of Kashmir, and who, on account of the bigoted assiduity with which he demolished the vestiges of Hindu superstition, is constantly alluded to by the title *But Skeken,* the idol breaker. Gopaditya, after a reign of 60 years, was succeeded by his son Gokarna,[60] of whom it is merely stated that he erected a temple to Gokarneswara.[61] Narendraditya,[62] his son, succeeded him, after a reign of 57 years; he reigned 31 years and a few months and left the crown to his son Yudhisthira[63] surnamed the blind, from the smallness of his eyes.

B. C. 216 or 40. The commencement of this monarch's reign was influenced by the same attention to virtue and propriety, as had governed the conduct of his pious predecessors. As fortune

[56] Kutnund. Vistnund. Nir. Aj.—*Ain-i-Akbari.* [57] Kulvarit—*Ibid*

[58] Bedia-ud-din notices a tradition that the tomb in this building was said to enshrine the remains of a Christian apostle.

[59] This is from Rafiuddin, but Narayan Kul asserts that it was still standing in his time. Forster does not notice any ruins or buildings on this spot, but we have mention made of them by Bernier. "There is another mountain opposite this one which has a small mosque with a garden and a very ancient building which appear to have been a temple of idols, which is why it is called *Takht-i-Suleman,* Suleman's Throne, vol. ii. p. 274. (Fr. original: *Le trone de Souleman*).

[60] Kurren.—*Ain-i-Akbari.*

[61] The lord of Gokarna, being in fact a Linga, as whenever that emblem of Siva is set up, it receives the appellation of Iswara compounded with some word expressive of the divine attributes, as Visweswara, the Lord of all; of the locality of its site, as Gangeswara, Kedareswara, &c. or of the person by whom it is erected, as in the text.

[62] Nurundrawut.—*Ain-i-Akbari.* [63] Jewdishter—*Ibid.*

had however decreed that he should be the last of his dynasty, he gradually ceased to regard the lessons of prudence and piety, and addicted himself to sensual pleasures and disgraceful society; he was constantly inebriated with wine; his companions were harlots and buffoons, and he treated with levity and scorn the admonition of his counsellors; the administration of affairs was neglected; the chief nobles defied the royal authority, and foreign princes encroached upon the confines of the kingdom. To prevent the ruin of the state, and to revenge upon the prince the insults they had received or prevent those which they anticipated, the ministers approached the palace with a numerous and well appointed force; as resistance was hopeless, the king precipitately fled from Srinagar, and secreted himself in the woods and mountains with his women and a few followers, doomed now to exchange luxury for privation, the downy couch for the sharp rock, and the harmony of minstrels for the wild dashing of cascades, or the wilder horns of the mountaineers; he at last found a refuge in the court of some compassionate princes, where, according to general belief he died in exile; according to other accounts, he engaged in unsuccessful attempts to recover his kingdom, in one of which he was taken prisoner by the nobles and thrown into captivity, from which he was released only by his death. The term of his reign was 48 years.

B. C. 168 or 10. The successor of Yudhisthir was Pratapaditya,[64] who was invited from another country; he was a kinsman of the king Vikramaditya; a different monarch, says our author, from the Sakari Vikramaditya, although sometimes identified erroneously with that prince;[65] he was a virtuous monarch and enjoyed a prosperous reign of 32 years, leaving his crown to his son, Jalaukas,[66] who also reigned 32 years, and was succeeded by his son Tunjina[67] who with his queen Vakpushta erected the temple of Tungeswara, and founded the city Haravasantika, in a district watered by the Satahrada and Payovaha like the bow of Indra, and its string.[68] In their time existed Chandaka, a portion of Dwaipayana, whose *Natya* is well known.

[64] Pertaubdut—*Ain-i-Akbari.*

[65] Notwithstanding our author's assertion, it seems probable that the identification is right. Narayan Kul and Bedia-ud-din state that Pratapaditya was related to Vikramaditya, the celebrated prince of Malwa; we shall have occasion to advert hereafter to this subject more fully.

[66] Juggook—*Ain-i-Akbari.* [67] Bunjir—*Ain-i-Akbari.*

[68] The first is the Sutlej, the second must be the Beyah, to which the name in the text sufficiently approaches.

In the reign of this prince an unseasonable fall of snow in the month of Bhadra destroyed the crops and caused a famine, in which great numbers of people perished; such was the general distress, that all the ties of society were dissolved and all the duties of life disregarded; modesty and pride, family honour, and public respect were all forgotten; the love of parent and child, of husband and wife, no longer prevailed; every individual sought alone for self-preservation, and although reduced to bones and tendons, the famished skeletons fought with fury for the carcases of the dead.

The king exerted himself to relieve the distresses of his subjects, and exhausted his own treasures, as well as those of his ministers, in procuring supplies of grain; the jewels of his court and queen were appropriated to the same purpose, but the famine still continuing, the monarch, despairing of relieving his afflicted people, and unable to witness their sufferings, determined to put a period to his existence by committing his body to the flames; from this purpose he was dissuaded by his queen, and once more addressing their earnest supplications to the gods, they obtained by their divine interposition, a miraculous shower of pigeons, who fell dead in the streets of the capital every day for a considerable period, and furnished the inhabitants with food until the products of the earth once more supplied them with subsistence. This prince died after a reign of 36 years, his wife accompanied him on the funeral pile at a place thence called Vakpushtatavi, and to which it was customary, in our author's time, for persons to bring the dead bodies of those husbands to be burnt, whose wives had the virtue to emulate the example of this pious princess. As the pure piety of this couple did not permit their having posterity, a prince of another family ascended the throne: he was named Vijaya,[69] and built the temple of Vijayeswara in the capital. He reigned 8 years, and was succeeded by his son.

Jayendra,[70] who was distinguished by the length of his arms, his hands touching his knees; this prince was fortunate at first in a minister of great integrity and talent, named Sandhimati, but influenced by the advice of those who envied the minister's superiority, the king conceived an aversion for him, and dismissed him from his employments; the poverty to which he was thus reduced served only to heighten his reputation; he devoted all his thoughts to religion, but a report, of heavenly origin, soon

[69] Bejeery.—Abul Fazl.

[70] Chunder—*Ibid.*

prevailed that he was yet destined to wear a crown; when the report reached the king, his fears were excited, and seizing the person of Sandhimati he threw him into prison, and kept him several years in close confinement; at the expiration of that term, the king, feeling his end approaching, was determined before his death to frustrate the decrees of fate, and to carry with him into a future state the spirit of his obnoxious minister. Accordingly, on the same night on which the monarch's body was burnt, the executioners put Sandhimati to death upon a stake.[71] Jayendra reigned 37 years.

When Isana, the Guru of Sandhimati, heard of his death, he repaired to the place of execution, to recover the body, and secure for it funeral rites. On taking the body from the stake, and fastening the feet and head together, in order to remove the corpse more commodiously, he was struck by an inscription on the forehead, which his knowledge enabled him to decipher; it was to this effect, "a life of poverty, ten years' imprisonment, death on a stake, and accession to a throne", predictions of which three had come to pass, and the fourth was yet to be fulfilled. For the accomplishment of the splendid part of our hero's fate, the Brahman performed those rites which compel the attendance of the ministers of Siva, the Yoginis; who accordingly appeared, and restored animation to the lifeless body of Sandhimati, whom they endowed with singular beauty and supernatural powers, and hailed as future king by the title of Arya Raja.[72] The news of this miraculous restoration spread through the kingdom, and all classes of people, impelled by resistless destiny, hastened to salute him as king; they led him in triumph to the capital, and he commenced his pious reign.

Whoever might have been the person, thus made the subject of miraculous tradition, it appears from our author's account, supported by him by reference to local corroboration, that he was an active promoter of the worship of Siva as the Linga, with the usual accompaniments of the trident and the bull. Many

[71] *kruraih vadhakarmadhikaribhih sandhimatih sule samaropya vi (vya) paditah...*
"Sandhimati being elevated by the savage executioners on the Sula was killed." He was perhaps impaled. Wilford however considers the instrument to be a cross. See *Asiatic Researches*, vol. x. But the punishment of impaling has always prevailed in the east; accounts of it in Ceylon, Java, Burma &c are numerous and authentic.

[72] Ariraj.—Abul Fazl.

temples of this description, continued at a long subsequent period, to be ascribed to this reign, and particularly one called Sahasralingam, from its containing a thousand Lingas, constructed of stone, the remains of which were visible in the time of Kalhana Pandit.

After reigning 47 years, Arya, the pious monarch, whose court was like the palace of Maheswara, where the articles of fashionable dress were ashes of burnt cowdung, rosaries of the Eleocarpus, and matted locks of hair, and the favourites and companions of the prince were mendicants and ascetics, grew weary of the cares of state, and determined to retire into the seclusion, better suited to his apparently fanatical propensities; having found that a descendant of Yudhishthir still lived, he recommended the youth as his successor, and delivering the government into the hands of the nobles, he divested himself of his royal ornaments, and with no other garment than the *Dhoti,* barefooted, and without his turban, carrying with him the Archalinga,[73] and observing a strict silence, he came out from the city, followed by an immense concourse of people. At the end of about two miles he sat down under a tree, and addressed his followers, whom he prevailed upon to disperse; he then resumed his route to the Tirtha of Nandisa or Nandikshetra, where he ended his days in ascetic mortification, and the assiduous worship of the god whom the three worlds obey.

Meghavahana,[74] who was invited to succeed to the throne of his ancestors, was the third in descent from Yudhisthir, being his great grandson : his father had found an asylum at the court of Gopaditya, king of Gandhara, whose assistance had restored him to some degree of opulence and consequence. His son Meghavahana was thence enabled to present himself amongst the candidates for the hand of the princess of Pragjyotish or Assam and to obtain her election.[75] With his wife, and a suitable dower, he had rejoined his father, when the Nobles of Kashmir sent a

[73] The Jangam profess the exclusive worship of Siva, and an appropriate emblem of that deity,...... inclosed in a diminutive silver or copper shrine or temple, is suspended from the neck of every votary as a sort of personal god.—Wilks's *Mysore*, i. p. 501. This is probably the Archalingam of our original, *archa* meaning worship. The introduction of this sect into the Dakshin in the eleventh century must have been long subsequent to its establishment in the north of India, by any calculation that may be adopted.

[74] Magdahan—Abul fazl.

[75] According to Bedia-ud-din the lady was the princess of Khota.

deputation to solicit and accompany his return to that kingdom, to which he immediately hastened, and of which he assumed the sovereignty.

Meghavahana, although a worshipper of the orthodox divinities, was inclined to adopt the Buddhist doctrine ; he encouraged the professors of that heresy to settle in his dominions, and particularly prohibited the destruction of animal life, granting from the public revenue a maintenace to such individuals as followed the business of hunters or butchers, whom his enactments deprived of their accustomed means of support.

Although thus careful of brute existence, he seems to have been less scrupulous about human life ; being a warlike and victorious sovereign, and engaging in remote and hostile expeditions he is said to have led his armies to the sea shore, and by the aid of Varuna, who opened a dry path through the waters for his army, to have crossed over to Lanka, where he ascended, with his troops, the gem-enshrining peak of the mountain Rohana.[76] Whilst encamped on the mountain, the king of the island, the Rakshasa Vibhishana,[77] came voluntarily, and submitted to his invader, in consequence of which he was confirmed in his sovereignty, on condition of his no longer permitting in his island the expenditure of animal life.[78] Meghavahana then returned to Kashmir, where the memory of his transmarine expedition, says our Sans-

[76] Adam's peak the *Rahu* and *Rahun* of the Muhammadans, according to whom also it contained mines of precious gems. Rohana implies the act or instrument of ascending as steps, a ladder, &c. and may refer to the rude steps and links of iron chain work, described by Valentyn, and more recently by Percival, and Sir William Ouseley, vol. i. p. 59.

[77] After the defeat and death of Ravana, Rama conferred the sovereignty of Lanka upon Ravana's younger brother Vibhishana, who is generally supposed to be still the monarch of Lanka.

[78] In other words, he introduced or enforced the Buddhist faith. Whatever credit it may be thought, that these Kashmirian tales of a conquest of Ceylon by one of their kings deserve, they are curiously connected with the Sinhalese traditions of foreign invasion, and consequent introduction of Buddhism. Vijaya Raja, the first monarch of that island, and who introduced the present religion, invaded it, it is said either 534 years before Christ, or A. D. 77 or 106 or 350.—*Asiatic Researches,* vol. vii. pp. 51 and 421, Molony and Joinville's Accounts of Ceylon.—Discordances that admit perhaps of some explanation, the first referring to the period at which Gautama the founder of Buddhism existed, and the others to the date of its introduction in the Island, an event to which foreign conquest was chiefly conducive.

3

krit guide, is still preserved on the banners, which on particular occasions, are carried before the kings of Kashmir.

The son of the last prince, Sreshtasena,[79] also called Pravarasena, succeeded his father : the Hindu record only commemorates his founding a temple of Pravaresa : but Bedia-ud-din makes considerable additions to his history; according to him, this prince established his mother on the vacant throne of Khota, and extended his own authority to Khatai, Chin and Machin. He reigned 30 years, and left his kingdom to his two sons Hiranya[80] and Toramana, the former holding the superior station of the *Samrajya,* and the latter that of the *Yauvarajya,* or being respectively Emperor and Cæsar, a division of power of considerable antiquity amongst the Hindus, and one which, with them, as well as with the Latin, Greek, or German princes, was often a source of public contention; it proved to be so in the instance before us : The latter having proceeded to strike coins[81] in his own name, the elder brother took offence at the measure, and deposed the Yuvaraja, and kept him in close confinement. The wife of Toramana, who was pregnant at the time, effected her escape, and found shelter and privacy in a potter's cottage, where she was delivered of a son; the boy was brought up by the potter as his own, but his high birth betrayed itself, and he was a prince in all his sports and amongst his playfellows; his juvenile imperiousness having caught the attention of Jayendra, his maternal uncle, then searching for his sister, led

[79] Sareshsain—Abul fazl

[80] Heren—*Ibid.*

[81] *Dinars* : the word is Sanskrit, and although generally signifying a certain weight of gold also means as above, a gold coin perhaps of the weight of 32 ratis or about 40 grains. The Dinar must have been common in Persia and Syria at the time of the Arabic invasion, as the Arabs to whom an original coinage was then unknown, adopted both it and the Dirhem or Drachma. According to the *Ain-i-Akbari,* the Dinar weighs one miscal, and is equal to 1 and 3/7th of a Dirhem, which weighs from 10 to 5 miscals, or, at 7½, the average giving a proportion of gold and silver, as 1 to 10. According to Ferishta the Dinar was worth Rs. 2, which will give us about the same proportion. There is an evident etymological affinity between the Dinar of the Hindus and the Denarius of the Romans; the latter, though originally a silver coin, was also of gold, and the author of the Periplus named Adrian's, states, that Denarii, both gold and silver, were amongst the articles exported from Europe and carried to Barygaza or Baroach; the Sanskrit, Dinar, may therefore be derived from the Roman coin.

to their discovery, and that nobleman privately took home his sister and her son. In the meantime Toramana died in captivity; on which event the princess, to divert her grief, went, accompanied by her son upon a pilgrimage to the south. During her absence the king died, after a reign of thirty years and two months. He left no posterity, and the claims of his nephew being unknown, the throne of Kashmir was vacant, and continued so for a short period.

The ruler of Ujjain at that time was Sriman Harsha Vikramaditya, who after expelling the *Mlechhas* and destroying the Sakas, had established his power and influence throughout India.[82]

In his train was a Brahman named Matri Gupta, to whom he was much attached. Upon hearing of the vacant situation of the Kashmir throne, and the indecision of the nobles with regard to a successor, he sent the Brahman to them, with a letter from himself recommending him to their election. They complied with the recommendations of a sovereign, whose commands they felt themselves unable to resist, and crowned Matri Gupta[83] as their king.

The reign of the Brahman was of limited duration; the death of his powerful protector exposed him to the disaffection of his chief subjects, and to the arms of the lawful heir Pravarasena, who with a small but resolute band of friends was approaching Kashmir. He seems to have surprised the Brahman by an unexpected attack upon his camp, or at least to have encountered him upon a journey when unprepared for a contest, and

[82] Who was this prince? As the enemy of the Sakas, and also from our author's chronology, he is synchronous with Salivahana, with whom indeed, notwithstanding a difference in date of 135 years, all the Hindu accounts represent him to have been engaged in hostility. We have had a Vikramaditya before him in this history, not the Sakari as expressly remarked by the historian, and therefore we cannot doubt our author's meaning, although we may question his chronological correctness, as I shall hereafter endeavour to show; it is singular that in a very long eulogium on this prince, which I have not thought it necessary to translate, the author never alludes to Salivahana, nor to any of the literary ornaments usually assigned to Vikrama's court. The name Harsha appears to bear some affinity to Harsha Megha (*Asiatic Researches*, vol. ix. p. 175) father of the Vikrama of the fifth century, in which indeed he may not very improbably be placed. We must however leave these points for the present, as we are not yet prepared for their due discussion. The Muhammadan writers are of no assistance here, as they repeat the name of Vikramajit without any comment on its again occurring.

[83] Mater kunt—Abul fazl.

although no serious engagement ensued, the issue was Matri Gupta's abdication of the throne and his departure to Banaras, where he passed the rest of his life in religious duties ; he reigned four years and nine months.

A. D. 123—476. Pravarasena,[84] so named after his grandfather, to whose dominion he had succeeded, was an active and enterprising prince ; he invaded the kingdoms of the south and turned his arms against the son and successor of Vikramaditya, named Pratapasila or Siladitya,[85] whom he drove from his capital, and took prisoner. He seems to have been contented with this expression of his resentment, and not only to have spared the life of the prince, but put him again in possession of his hereditary kingdom, carrying off however the throne of the Apsarasas, which he transferred to his own capital.[86] After his return he determined to found a city which should be the capital of his kingdom, and he accordingly constructed the city of Srinagar,[87] on the banks of the Vitasta, and embellished it with many palaces and

[84] Pirwirsein—Abul fazl.

[85] I have not been able yet to trace this son of Vikrama in any other works with much success. Wilford informs me that in the *Kshetra Samasa* it is stated that Vikramaditya had a son named Natha Sila whom he is disposed to regard as the grandson of Vikrama, and the son of this Siladitya. A Jain work of some celebrity, the *Satrunjaya Mahatmya*, is said to have been written by order of Siladitya, king of Surat ; the author Dhaneswara Suri, according to a marginal note in the copy I consulted, and which agrees with the traditionary opinion of the Jains, wrote his work in the Samvat year 477. The same work cites a prophetic annunciation, that the famous Vikramaditya would appear after 466 years of his era had elapsed (*Asiatic Researches*, vol. ix. p. 142), which scarcely agrees with the date assigned for the work, as, if Siladitya, the son of Vikramaditya, succeeded his father, it allows but ten years for the reign of the latter. We must revert to this hereafter.

[86] The famous throne supported by thirty-two female images, animated ones, if we are to believe the legend. Accounts agree of its being lost after Vikrama's death, although it is generally thought to have been found again by Bhoja. We have no further notice of it in our history. Bedia-ud-din carries Pravarasena to Bengal also, where he subdues Behar Singh, ruler of Dhacca, and gives the Government to Palas Singh, son of Siladitya, a son of the author's, making apparently the words Palas and Dhac, implying the same thing, a sort of tree.

[87] "The city, which in the ancient annals of India was known by the name of Serinaghar, but now by that of the province at large, extends about three miles on each side of the river Jhelum, over which are four or five wooden bridges."—Forster, vol. ii. p. 9.

temples; he also threw a bridge across the river. His being the founder of this city is confirmed by the Muhammadan writers, although, as one of them observes, it has undergone many vicissitudes since the period of its foundation. Pravarasena reigned 63 years.

A. D. 186-499 and 237-545. The successors of this prince were his son Yudhishthir, who reigned thirty-nine years and three months, and his son Narendraditya, or Lakshmana,[88] who ruled thirteen years; he was succeeded by his younger brother, to whose reign the extravagant period of 300 years is assigned, an extravagance the more remarkable, as it is without a parallel in our author's chronology,[89] and which must therefore have been suggested, either by a necessity for filling up some dark chasm in the annals of Kashmir, or to compensate for an error in the dates of the preceding monarchs, who may have been placed two or three centuries too soon; both causes may perhaps have united for this extraordinary departure from those bounds of possibility, which in all other reigns have been preserved.

The length of Ranaditya's reign is not the only marvel attached to that prince; he had been in fact, in his former life, a man of dissipated habits, but at last, by his devotion to Bhramaravasini, a form of Durga, obtained, as a reward, his resuscitation in a royal race, and the goddess herself as a consort, incarnate as Ranarambha, the daughter of Roti Sena, king of Chola.[90] The divine nature of his queen was the immediate cause of the king's protracted reign, as she conferred upon him the Patala Siddha Mantra, by which he was enabled to extend his life as along as he pleased. At last, however, satiated with this world, he entered the cave of Namuchi, in the bed of the Chandrabhaga river, through which he passed to Patala, and acquired a kingdom in the infernal regions; his wife regarded rather inconsistently as a Sakti of Vishnu, went upon her husband's death to Swetadwipa.

A. D. 537-568 & 579-592. The claims of the next monarch to the throne of Kashmir are not stated by our original,

[88] Jewdishter. Lekhmen. Zebadut.—Abul fazl.

[89] Unlike the early periods of the Persian Chronicles, in which such a term is far from uncommon.

[90] The traditions of the South intimate occasional connexions of a like character between the Chola and Kashmir princes. One of the former entitled in one account Sasi Sekhara and in another Rajadhi Raja Chola was married, it is said, to a daughter of the king of Kashmir.

and the enumeration of his genealogical progenitors warrants a suggestion that he might not have the immediate successor of Ranaditya : he was the son of Vikrameswara the son of Vikramakranta Viswa, and is named himself Vikramaditya, a strange series of appellations, and a further proof of some unaccountable blank in the Kashmirian records : Vikramaditya reigned 42 years and was succeeded by his younger brother Baladitya.[91]

Baladitya was a prince of a warlike character, and erected his pillars[92] of victory on the shores of the eastern sea ;[93] one result of his victorious excursions was his compelling the subjugated monarches to beautify Kashmir, and to construct temples and edifices for the accommodation of such of their subjects, as might visit that kingdom.[94]

It was foretold to this prince by an astrologer, that he should be the last of the race of Gonarda, and his only daughter should transfer the kingdom to a different dynasty of princes.[95] The monarch was not well pleased with this prediction and resolved

[91] Beckermadut.—Baladut.—Abul fazl. The Muhammadan writers agree with the text except Bedia-ud-din ; he assigns a life of 165 years to this monarch, and a reign of no more than 40 years : he places also the 30th year of his reign as contemporary with the first of the Hijra, and describes his sending an ambassador to Mohammed.

[92] Jayastambha, the Pillars of Sesak and the Trophies of the Greeks and Romans. That it was the custom of Hindu princes to erect these pillars is established by concurrent testimonies, and it is probable that it is to this practice we are to ascribe the origin of several solitary stone columns still met with in India, as the Lat of Firoz-shah, the Kutab Minar, the pillar at Allahabad, and those in Tirhut, and other places ; in general however they were constructed, like the wooden trophies of the Greeks, of less durable materials, and as observed by Plutarch, "Time has gradually effaced these memorials of national hostility."

[93] I am especially afraid of my manuscript here : it is alone, in this section of the history, and is very inaccurate. It is said that this prince conquered Bankala or Bengal, a very uncommon name, however, in Hindu books of any period, Gaur or Banga being the usual term.

[94] Consistently with the former chronology Bedia-ud-din makes this prince contemporary with Yezdejird, from whom he wrested the north eastern districts of Persia, but he confounds Baladitya with Pratapaditya here, and passes over the intermediate monarch altogether.

[95] We have seen however the crown repeatedly pass into different families, and therefore our author nods ; unless indeed he considered the princes so described, as members, not of a different race, but of other branches of the Gonardiya stock.

to prevent its fulfilment by refusing to grant his daughter in marriage at all ; his precautions were unavailing.[96] A descendant of Karkota Naga and protege of the monarch, succeeded in obtaining privately the affections and person of the princess, and the assistance of the chief officers of state secured his accession to the throne, upon the death of the king, which happened shortly afterwards.[97]

[96] Elsewhere (see p. 38), Wilson refers to "some unaccountable blank in Kashmirian records." As a matter of fact, the Book I of Kalhana's *Rajatarangini* deals at the outset with four kings—Gonanda I, Damodara I, Yasovati and Gonanda II—after which the records of 35 kings are lost.—Ed.

[97] Gonanda or Gonarda (See footnote 12, p. 14), the first king of Kashmir, according to Kalhana, was contemporaneous with the battle of *Mahabharata*, the date of which event he fixes at 653rd year of Kali. He rejects the opinion held by some that it took place at the end of Dvapara. Now the reigns of the kings whose history is known, covered a period of 2,330 years, up to the time of Kalhana Pandit, and those of the fifty-two kings whose history is not known covered a period of 1,266 years, making a total of 3,596 years, between the time of the first king of Kashmir and Kalhana. But the first king, Gonanda or Gonarda, lived in 653 of the Kali Yuga, hence Kalhana lived in the year 4,249th of Kali—See *Rajatarangini*—J. C. Dutt's translation, vol-1, Appendix A.—Ed.

CHAPTER II

A. D. 616. Durlabha Vardhana,[1] the descendant of Karkota,[2] thus obtained the princess and the kingdom, and founded a new and powerful dynasty. His reign was chiefly distinguished by his encouragement of religion, and the temples he founded, or the endowments he bestowed upon the Brahmans. He reigned 36 years and was succeeded by his son.

A. D. 652. Pratapaditya[3] was the founder of Pratapapur converted by local pronunciation into Tapar, according to the Muhammadan authorities. In this new city a merchant named Nona, of the Rauhitya race, took up his abode, and founded a college for the residence of Rauhitya Brahmans. Of the wealth of the trader it is stated as a proof, that on one occasion he lighted up his house with diamonds to receive the king, whom he had heard formerly complain of being inconvenienced by the smoke of the ordinary lamps. The familiarity between the prince and merchant led to some unexpected results. The former fell deeply in love with one of the merchant's women, and being unwilling either to commit a breach of hospitality, or to forfeit his fair name by a vicious act, he struggled with his passion and endeavoured to subdue it. The contest induced a fever, which threatened his life; he was saved however by the generosity of his friend, who learning the cause of his disease, not only yielded up the woman to the king, but exerted no small ingenuity in argument to persuade him to accept her. His logic however, made a due impression, and Narendra Prabha was elevated to the royal bed. It was a fruitful one, as she bore the king seven sons, Chandrapira, Tarapira, Abhimuktapira, Amuktapira, Vajraditya, Udayaditya and Lalitaditya, several of whom succeeded in time to the crown. Pratapaditya died after a reign of 50 years.

A. D. 702. Chandrapira,[4] the eldest son and successor of the last monarch, was a prince of exemplary mildness and equity. He punished his own officers, for encroaching on the tenements of

[1] Dirleyir Dirwun—Abul fazl.

[2] Karkota is one of the Nagas or serpent demigods. The name occurs, as well as Nila, in the list of them in the *Mahabharata;* A temple at Banaras is also dedicated to this serpent deity.

[3] Pertaubadut—Abul fazl.

[4] Chandranund.—Abul fazl.

a *chamar*,[5] or worker in leather, in preparing the site of a temple which he wished to erect, and which design he was prepared to abandon if the consent of the leather-worker could not be obtained. A liberal reward and his personal solicitation obtained the acquiescence of the *Chamar*. His ground was duly made over to the king, and the temple was completed. We have another legend of his equity and discrimination respecting the means employed by him to detect the murderer of a Brahman, but it need not be here repeated, as the story has been told by Abul fazl.[6] Chandrapira enjoyed the short reign of no more than eight years and eight months, and was succeeded by his brother Tarapira,[7] a violent and oppressive sovereign, and an enemy of the priesthood;

[5] Who as an out-caste could have no rights under a strict Hindu administration.

[6] *Ain-i-Akbari*, ii. 175. I do not find in my copies, the description of the punishment awarded. Abul fazl says the murderer was branded in the forehead with the figure of a headless man, and that something of the kind was inflicted appears from the context, from which a stanza has been probably omitted; The punishment is according to law, which on no account permits the infliction of capital punishment on the person of a Brahman, but substitues brands, exile and disgrace.

In the *Danda Viveka* the Law is thus laid down from ancient authorities:

mahapatakayuktopi na viprovadhamarhati
nirvasananka maundyam tasya kuryannaradhipah—Vrhaspati

A Brahman guilty of the greatest crimes is not to be put to death; let the king have him shaved, branded or exiled.—*Vrihaspati.*

brahmanasya bhrunahatya gurutalpa suvarnasteya surapaneshu
kabandha bhagasvapada dhvajastaptenayasena lalate'nkayitva
svavishayante nirvasanam—Baudhayanah

A Brahman who causes abortion, defiles the bed of his teacher, steals gold, or drinks spirits, must be branded with a hot iron on the forehead, with a headless figure, the vulva, the foot of a dog, or a flag, (the vintner's sign) and then be banished.—*Baudhayana.*

asirah purushah karyo lalate dvijaghatinah
gurutalpe bhagah karyah surapane suradhvajah
steyetu svapadam krtva sikhipittena purayet.—Naradah

A headless man is to be stamped on the forehead (of a Brahman) who kills a Brahman; the vulva on his who defiles his Guru's bed; a flag on his who drinks wine, and the foot of a dog on his who commits theft: filling the scar with *Sikhipitta* (Peacock's bile, or possibly some caustic substance.)—*Narada.*

[7] Taranand.—Abul fazl.

his reign was fortunately a limited one, and extended to no more than four years and a few days.

A third brother Lalitaditya[8] succeeded to the crown; he was a prince of great celebrity, and established by the vigour and success of his arms, his claims to the supreme sovereignty of India, having made with his victorious armies the triumphant circuit of Hindustan. His first scene of action was the Antarvedi country, the diadem of which he placed upon his own head. He then turned his arms against Yasovarma, at that time sovereign of Kanouj, a prince distinguished for his literary accomplishments, and the patronage extended by him to such eminent poets, as Kavivakpati, Rajasri and Bhavabhuti.[9] A peace was soon agreed upon between the monarchs but as speedily violated : some informality in the address of a dispatch from Yasovarma to Lalitaditya having excited the latter's resentment, led to a renewal of hostilities, and the total subversion of the kingdom of Kanouj.

Although thus occupied in foreign war, the prince appears to have devoted some attention to the details of domestic administration, and to have made a new arrangement of the great offices of his court. Over the eighteen branches of the governent he instituted five principal departments—the Mahapratiharapira, or office of high chamberlain, Mahasandhivigraha, that of chief minister, or supreme administrator of peace and war, Mahaswasala, of the royal stables, or of master of the horse, Mahabhandagara, or the high keeper of the treasury or arsenal, or perhaps both ; and the Mahasadhanabhaga, an office of which the nature is not fully conveyed by the nomenclature, but which may perhaps be the supreme directorial or executive administration. Sahi and others were the officers invested with these high functions.

[8] Lultadut.—Abul fazl.

[9] The two former of these are unknown. The third is celebrated as the author of the *Malati Madhava*, and the *Uttara Rama Charita*. He might have been at the court of Kunouj, but he was of a Berar or Vidarbha family ; he is usually considered as contemporary with Kalidasa, and in the *Bhoja Prabandha* is brought to Bhoja's court. His own works however afford no reason to suppose that he was contemporary with either Kalidasa, or Bhoja, and with respect to the latter, furnish grounds for inferring the prior date of the Poet. The *Rajatarangini* is therefore probably correct in placing him about A. D. 705 or nearly two centuries before the probable period of Bhoja's reign. Yasovarma himself is not known, unless he be the same with Kirtivarma, an appellation of like import, and a prince who is mentioned in the opening of the *Prabodha Chandradaya*.

Yasovarma, after the subjugation of his kingdom, fled across the Jamuna, and nothing more is mentioned of his history. His victorious antagonist followed up his success by an expedition to the shores of the eastern sea. Thence marching through Kalinga, the royal elephants advanced upon the kingdom of Gaur, and effected its subjugation. Lalitaditya thence proceeded southwards and invaded Karnata, then subject to a queen named Ratta, who submitted to the invader, after having seen her strongholds, in the Vindhya mountains unavailing to resist him. Her submission having disarmed the king's resentment, her beauty secured his favour, and she was restored to her dominions. The army then marched to the banks of the Kaveri, whence crossing the Sandal mountains, the king subdued the coast and the Islands opposite. Having reduced the seven Kramakas and seven Konkanas, Lalitaditya continued to follow the shores of the western sea to Dwaraka, which he entered to the delight of his soldiers : he then crossed the Vindhya mountains and occupied Avanti, whence having made the circuit of India, and received the homage of its numerous princes, he now directed his steps to the north. His march was a series of conflicts and triumphs. He was successively assailed by the princes of the country, like another Indra enaged in clipping the wings of the hostile hills. The studs of Kamboja were vacated at his approach, and Bukhara was deserted by its high-crested steeds. After three successful battles in as many days, he respected the Musalmans, and directed his attention to other quarters.[10] The pale-faced Bhotias scarcely attracted his regard, as the cold wind impregnated with the blossoms of the safflower, and the secretion of the musk deer, fanned the tresses of his soldiers. The city of Pragiyotish was empty on his arrival, and he turned thence to the Stri-Rajya, where the queen and her subjects triumphed over the monarch and his soldiers, by other weapons than those of war; after a short delay in that country, he advanced to the realms of Uttara Kuru, whence satiate with glory and laden with plunder he returned to his own dominions.[11]

[10] Bedia-ud-din carries him into Khorasan to aid Yezdejird, but he retreats before the fame of the Arab invaders.

[11] Whatever may be the truth of the military excursion of this Prince, the account of it given in the original, which has been here followed as closely as the state of the manuscript would admit, is a very curious specimen of the author's geographical accuracy and knowledge, and throws some light upon the state of India at the period at which he wrote. It may therefore be worthwhile to revise his track. From Kanouj

On his return to Kashmir Lalitaditya rewarded his principal officers by bestowing upon them subordinate kingdoms; in this way he conferred upon his dependants the principal cities of Jalandhara and Lahora (Lahore). He also devised particular marks through the eastern districts of the present company's possessions, Lalitaditya may be supposed to have marched to the delta of the Ganges, and Brahmaputra, where we have what our author calls the Eastern Sea; and the coast along the upper part of the Bay of Bengal, therefore, constitutes the country that he calls Kalinga, whence a slight deviation to the right brings him easily to Gaur, equivalent in its widest sense. to the greater part of modern Bengal. The transit hence to Karnata is rather a considerable stride, although it is obvious that the upper part of the Peninsula is intended, by reference to the *Durgas* of the Vindhya chain of mountains, unless indeed we extend the term to the eastern Ghats, which may be considered as lateral processes from the main ridge. As indeed the next stage is the Kaveri river, we come then to the southern limits usually assigned to the ancient Karnata kingdom. The Sandal or Malaya mountains are the western Ghats, over which as the king marched from Mysore he would necessarily come into the Konkan, the seven divisions of which, as well as the seven Kramukas, are something new to us, although from the voyages of the two Arabians and of the early Portuguese and Dutch adventurers, we know, that the part of the Malabar coast was divided amongst a great number of petty sovereigns. The seven Konkanas are indeed known in the Dakhin still, and comprehend the whole of the Parasu Rama Kshetra, or the greater part of the Malabar coast : They are named Kerala (Malabar), Tulunga or Tuluva, Gova Rashtra or Goa, Konkana proper, Karataha, Varalatta and Barbara. The seven Kramukas, it might have been conjectured, were connected with the term Kranganore, but the original name of that province is properly written Korangalur (Kodangalur), and they possibly signify some of the groups of islands off the coast of Malabar; the island of Dwaraka, in Gujarat, the kingdom of Krishna, is the next stage, and was visited more in veneration than enmity; from hence across the Vindhya mountains the king comes to Ujjain; his march to the north, or rather northwest, brings him to Kamboja; according to Wilford (*Asiatic Researches*, vol. viii. p. 336) the ancient Arachosia, and unquestionably a country in that direction, a country bordering on India, to the northwest, and inhabited by impure or foreign tribes, famous also for its breed of horses, a large strong breed of which is still reared in the countries between Persia and India. Bhukhara is the Persian Bokhara or Bucharia; the word rendered in the text Musalman is written in the original Mussuni or Mussulli; it is intended by our author as the name of a person, for it occurs again in the reign of Lalitaditya's grandson Jayapira, who is said in the original to have had Mussuni and others as chiefs of his nocturnal guard. At the same time the recurrence of the name after to be borne by the different tribes as characteristic of their submission to his power. Thus the Turushkas were obliged to shave half the head, and the Dakhinis to let the ends of their waist cloth hang down like a tail behind, and these distinctions are still observed.[12] If he thus treated the vanquished with some contumely,

such an interval, indicates rather more than one individual, and is an argument in favour of its being a generic appellation; according to Narain Kul it should be Momunkhan, Governor or Prince of Bokhara. If he is right, it should be Al-maimun of the house of Abbas that is intended, and who long resided in Khorasan, but about a century after the reign of Lalitaditya, according to the chronology of our text. The correction that would thus be required does not however seem to be indispensable, as our author's history here, allowing for national partialities is very strongly supported by the general histories of the Mahammadan writers. At this very period, or from 697 to 712, the generals of Hijaz, the Governor of Khorasan, were engaged in active hostilities with their neighbours, both to the north and east, or in Bokhara and Kabul, the Hindu prince of which latter makes a distinguished figure in several transactions, (Price's *Mohammedan History*, vol i. p. 454 &c). Such a general coincidence is as much as can be expected, for names are most deplorably disfigured by both Hindu and Mahammadan writers, and events, especially when remote in place and time, are not investigated by either with much accuracy or care. Lalitaditya's next route through Bhutan is rather a remote one, except we suppose the name Bhuteas to be applied to the hill tribes on the northern side of the Himalaya. The route is practicable enough, and would be much the same as that followed by the Lamas in 1712, and by which a considerable intercourse between Kashmir and Chinese Tartary is still maintained, (see Moorcroft's *Travels*) : that the Bhuteas are scattered through this line we know from late authorities. Hamilton observes that the Bhuteas occupy everywhere between the hills and the Tista the Alpine region on both sides of the Indus, (Hamilton's *Nepal*, 58) and Fraser mentions that Hymap, a valley, containing a great number of Bhutea villages, is only four days' journey from the capital of Kashmir (Fraser's *Himala*, p. 308); however our author evidently intends to carry his hero in Bhutan proper, a journey of considerable extent although probably not so much so as it appears by the maps we yet possess. Pragjyotish is considered to be Gohati (*Gouhati*) in Assam, (*Asiatic Researches*, vol. viii. p. 336) the Stri Rajya is probably Tibet, where customs similar to those of the Malabar Nairs prevail, (Turner's *Embassy*, p. 349). It may however be Nepal or almost any portion of the Himalaya, (Kirkpatrick, p. 187, Fraser, p. 70 &c) where the same practice exists, but as the march leads off from Assam apparently to the north, we may regard this region to be Tibet. Of Uttara Kuru we shall have further occasion to speak.

12 The neighbouring Musalmans like most Mahammedans indeed,

he made amends by his munificence, for there was no part of India, where he did not erect statues and temples of the Gods. A very long enumeration ensues of these proofs of his liberality, of which it will here be necessary only to particularize a few. He founded the cities of Sunischitapura, Darpitapura, Phalapura, Lalitapura and Parihasapura. In Hushkapur he erected an image of Mukta Swami, and one of Nrihari in the Stri Rajya. In the Bhumi Grama he built the temple of Jyeshta Rudra, and over and along the Vitasta he built bridges and stone ghats. Prihasapura was his favorite work; in this city he built a palace of unhewn stone, and a variety of royal and religious edifices; he raised a column of one stone, 24 cubits long, and bearing on the summit an image of Garuda; he placed in the temples images of metal; one of Vishnu as Parihasa Kesava was made of pure silver, weighing 1000 palas, and another colossal figure of Buddha was constructed of 1000 Prasthas of brass; a figure of Hari with flowing hair, was set up of gold, and another golden image was made by him of the same deity in the Varaha Avatar. His example was imitated by his queens, by tributary princes, and by his ministers, one of whom, a second Jina, named Chankuna, a native of Bokhara, erected a Vihar, and set up in it an image made in Magadha or Bihar, called indifferently by our author Jina Vimba and Sugata Vimba, and therefore of undetermined character as to its being of Buddhist or Jaina manufacture, although

do shave the centre of the head still, and the people of the coast wear their lower garments long. That these habits were imposed by the kings of Kashmir may be denied even on Hindu authority. In the *Hari-Vamsa*, a portion of the *Mahabharata*, and certainly much older than the work before us, the following account is given of the imposition, of the distinguishing modes of wearing the hair, upon the tribes of *Mlechchas* or foreigners : "The king Sagara in obedience to the orders of his Guru, Vasishta, deprived the *Mlechchas* of their institutes, and imposed upon them these marks. The Sakas had half the head shaved, the Yavanas and Kambojas the whole of their hair taken off, the Paradas were ordered to wear beards." These customs might perhaps admit of verification, and might enable us to identify the tribes. Some of the Greeks were from a remote period accustomed to shave the forepart of the head; the mountaineers of the Himalaya shave the crown, as do the people of Kaferistan with the exception of a single tuft, and some of these people, which is a curious coincidence, are called Kaumojees, (Elephinstone's *Cabul*, pp. 619 and 625.) They also some of them wear beards five or six inches long. The Persians also wore long beards in the time of Ammianus Marcellinus, as they do still.

most probably the former. The foundation of Parihasapura,[13] or Parrispur and its embellishment by this prince are recorded by the Mahammedan writers, of whom Mohammad Azim adds that the fragments of the pillar of Garuda were visible in his time. The statue of Sugata also remained to the period in which our author wrote.

Lalitaditya is the subject of many marvellous stories, one of which reminds us of the exploit of Zopyrus. The minister of the king of Sikata Sindhu, probably of Tatta, presented himself in a wounded and deplorable state before the king, upon one of his expeditions. Lalitaditya took him into favour, in return for which he offered to lead the army across the desert, against his native country and his offer being accepted, he directed the king to provide water for a fortnight's march. At the expiration of the fortnight the army was still in the midst of the sands, and the men were perishing with thirst, the guide acknowledging that he had been employed by his sovereign to effect the destruction of the king and his host. The attempt of that enemy was foiled, however, by the discovery of some springs, and the king returned in safety to Kashmir, after punishing his treacherous guide; the springs then opened were said to exist in our author's time, and to form a considerable stream running to the north called Kunta-vahini.[14]

Lalitaditya, although the substantial proofs of his devotion left no doubt of his piety, was yet not free from faults. Amongst other defects he was addicted to wine, and in one of his drunken fits he ordered the city Pravarapura founded by Pravarasena to be burnt, that it might no longer emulate the splendour of his own capital. His orders were carried rigidly into effect, to his own deep regret when sobered—and as one proof of the sense he entertained of the transaction, he immediately issued positive commands, for his officers to disregard any mandates whatever, that he should promulgate whilst under the influence of wine.[15]

[13] Purrispur is mentioned in the *Ain-i-Akbari*, vol. ii. p. 159, with the addition that a lofty idolatrous temple stood there, which was destroyed by Sekander. Refi-ud-din also converts the column into the minarets of a temple.

[14] The story is but imperfectly told here, but the text is so corrupt that I should scarcely have ventured to select even the above, had I not been countenanced by Narain Kul, who translates the story in much the same way, altering the name of the country to Maruka (that is, a desert tract) on the ocean.

[15] So it was related to Trajan, who indulged in a similar propensity.

We have an account, in this part of Lalitaditya's reign, of some tumultuous affray having taken place in his capital, between the followers of different deities. The exact nature of it does not satisfactorily appear from the imperfect condition of the manuscripts, but there seems to have been a conflict between a number of Bengali pilgrims, who had come with their prince to visit a temple of Saraswati, and the people of the city. The former had made an image of Parihasa Hari, and broken one of Rama Swami, and to punish the latter act the citizens assailed them. The Bengalis appear to have had the advantage, as the desolated temple of Rama Swami continued to bear witness to their success, and the world was filled with the fame of the exploit; the author of the *Wakiat-i-Kashmir* calls the king of Gaur, Gosala, without however assigning any authority for the appellation.[16]

The death of Lalitaditya was worthy of his active reign; he resoloved to explore the uttermost limits of Uttara Kuru, the regions inhabited by the followers of Kuvera, and equally inaccessible to the steps of man, and the rays of the sun.[17] He accordingly marched northwards, crossing the mountains inhabi-

Vinolentium prudentia molliverat, cuari vetans jussa post longiores epulas. —Aurelius Victor.

[16] The same work speaks of it as a hostile incursion of the Bengalis, and Narain Kul has the same, ascribing that event to the design of revenging the death of their king, who had been invited publicly and privately put to death by Lalitaditya, one of whose faults, he says, was that of disregarding oaths and agreements, a not uncommon failing in princes of Lalitaditya's ambition. Bedia-ud-din agrees with the latter author. There may possibly be some connection between his transaction and what is recorded in the *Sankara Digvijaya* of the reformer Sankaracharya, who, it is said, visited Kashmir, and despite strenuous opposition, seated himself on the throne dedicated to the Most Learned, in the temple of Saraswati. The place corresponds, so probably does the date; names only may have been changed.

[17] This Hindu Cimmeria is of course the land of fable, but as far as it may be supposed to have a real prototype Uttara Kuru seems to imply the northern portion of Russian and Chinese Tartary. The name however appears to have been known nearer home, and to have been applied to the North Eastern portion of the Himalaya mountains. Ptolemy places in that position a nation called the Ottorocorœ amongst mountains of the same name, and Ammianus Marcellinus calls the same Opurocarra. It is not impossible however that they intend the northern part of Assam called Uttarakora, Uttarakola or Uttarakul. Lalitaditya probably perished amongst the chasms and snows of the Himalayas.

ted by the Damaras, whom he describes in a letter to his ministers as a fierce intractable race, lurking in caves and fortified passes, possessed of considerable wealth, and equally devoid of government or religion. In the same despatch he announces the probability of his not returning, for, he observes, there are no limits to the advance of the ambitious, as there is no return of the water, which the rivers, running into foreign countries, bear far away from its native springs. In consequence of this expectation, he directed the ministers to crown his son Kuvalayaditya, with which order they sorrowfully complied. The king's anticipations were realized; neither he nor his army ever returned, and their fate was never exactly known. Some reports say that he was slain in battle; others that he and his host were overwhelmed and lost in a heavy fall of snow in Aryanaka. Some persons believe that he burnt himself, whilst others credit the tales that carry him to the farthest north, to those climes that are easily accessible to the immortals only, and speak of the wonders there seen and performed by him, and the final destruction of him and his troops. Lalitaditya reigned 36 years and eight months; he was a popular prince, and much beloved by those about his person; his chief ministers were all deeply afflicted by his loss, and one of them, Mitra Sarma, disdaining to survive his master, drowned himself at the confluence of the Sindu and Vitasta.

A.D. 751. Kuvalayapira,[18] the son of Lalitaditya by Kamala Devi succeeded to his father; in the first days of his reign, apprehending the rebellion of his brother, a prince of a more active and violent temper, he put him and his mother Chakramardika into confinement; thus relived from the fear of domestic disturbances he began to contemplate foreign acquisitions, when he was diverted from his purpose by a change in the tenor of his reflections. Having been thrown into a paroxysm of fury by an act of unimportant disobedience, in one of his ministers, he reflected, when he became calm, upon the folly of yielding to the impulses of passion; his meditations extended farther, and convincing him of the futility of human power, and the shortness of human existence, he determined to exchange his kingly throne for the cell of an ascetic. Having adopted this determination, he withdrew to the mountain Dripatha, leaving, after a short reign of little more than a year, the crown to his brother Vajraditya.[19]

[18] Kulyanund—Abul fazl.

[19] Bijradut—*Ibid.*

This prince was of a cruel and abandoned character; he expended his paternal treasures upon sensual gratifications, and drained Parihasapura of its valuables and money, to purchase women for his harem. To raise money also he sold great numbers of his subjects to the *Mlechchhas,* and propagated through the country tenets and practices fit for them alone. Fortunately his reign was a short one, lasting only seven years.

Prithivyapira,[20] the elder son of Vajraditya, by the queen Manjarika, succeeded his father, both in the throne and in his habits of life; at the end of four years, however, he was dethroned by his brother Sangramapira, the son of Mamma, one of Vajraditya's concubines apparently; this prince reigned seven years, and was succeeded by his younger brother.

A. D. 773. Jayapira,[21] was a monarch who was emulous of his grand-father Lalitaditya's, renown. Shortly after his accession, this prince marched upon an expedition against his neighbours. His army was numerous and well appointed, but not equally so with those which Lalitaditya had commanded, as a proof of which some of the elderly citizens observed to the king, who had questioned them on the subject, that he had but 80,000 litters with his army, whilst his grand-father had 125,000. He proceeded however on his expedition, and when he had marched some distance, Jajja[22] his wife's brother, availed himself of the opportunity to usurp the throne, and prepared for the maintenance of his unjust pretensions. Jayapira's first determination on receiving intelligence of the usurpation, was to march back to Kashmir, but on taking a review of his army, he found so many soldiers had deserted him, that he was not in a condition to vindicate his rights; he therefore disbanded the troops yet adhering to him, and with a few faithful followers retired to Prayaga where on arrival, he gave to the Brahmans the horses lately belonging to his army, amounting to 100,000 all but one, the grant declaring that whoever should give an entire lakh, might efface the seal of Jayapira, and substitute his own. This grant he committed to the Ganges, the waters of which were rendered purer by the ingredient; after a short residence at Allahabad he dismissed his attendants, and determined to seek his fortune by himself.

The adventures of Jayapira at Paundravardhana,[23] then the

[20] Pertooanund. Sungranund.—Abul fazl.

[21] Jeyanund.—*Ibid.*

[22] Jujnund.—*Ibid.*

[23] A city of Bihar, it is believed, but Magadha, in that case, must

residence of Jayanta, king of Gaur, are the next subjects of our original, and are narrated with a prolixity that we need not emulate; he arrived alone and in humble attire at the city, where his dignified person and manner attracted the notice of one of the female dancers of a temple, by whom he was taken home and supported; whilst in this situation he killed in private encounter a lion that had alarmed the whole city, and having in the conflict lost one of his bracelets, on which his name was inscribed, he was thence discovered by the emissaries of Jayanta, and carried before that monarch. His reception was highly favourable. Jayanta gave him his daughter in marriage, and furnished him with an army for the recovery of his paternal dominions, to which he was also invited by Deva Sarma, the son of Mitra Sarma, deputed for that purpose by the nobles of Kashmir; he accordingly set forth on his return, the goddess of victory in his van; and in his rear, the two terrestrial goddesses, Kalyananda, the princess his wife, and Kamala the dancer, whom out of gratitude he had also espoused. At a village called Sastikala on the borders of Kashmir, he was opposed by the usurper and a series of conflicts ensued without being attended, for several days, with any decisive result. At last Srideva, a Chandala, the headman of a village, who had joined the king, made his way to the spot where Jajja was stationed and struck him from off his horse with a stone. Jajja fell dead upon the field, his followers fled, and Jayapira after an interval of three years was again acknowledged as monarch of Kashmir.

The cares of Jayapira were now directed to the cultivation of letters and the improvement of his kingdom. He devoted much of his time to study and made himself proficient in Sanskrit Grammar, under Kshira, a learned teacher.[24] He invited

have been subject to the kings of Bengal, whose power about the time in question, the beginning of the ninth century, does appear to have been so extensive (see the Monghyar Grant, *Asiatic Researches*, Vol. i. p. 123 and Colebrooke's remarks on it, *Asiatic Researches* vol. ix. p. 427.) Jayanta however does not occur amongst the Pala princes, in those authorities, nor in Abul fazl's list (*Ain-i-Akbari*) unless in the latter some of the names are erroneous; a circumstance very probable.

[24] This name is not known unless Kshira Swami, the commentator on *Amara*, be intended; the conjecture is supported by the nature of his instruction and qualifications, the author calling him *savdavidyopadhyayah* or teacher of the science of words.

scholars from countries and so many flocked to him as to occasion a dearth of Pandits everywhere, except in Kashmir. The chief of the assembly was Bhatta and he was assisted by Damodara Gupta ; the principal poets were Manoratha, Sankhadanta, Chataka and Sandhiman, whilst Vamana and others were amongst his ministers.[25] The principal foundation of his reign was the fort of Jayapura in the construction of which he was assisted by artists sent him by Vibhishana, the Rakshasa monarch of Lanka, whilst Achu, the son-in-law of Pramoda king of Mathura, and Jayadatta one of the king's principal ministers, contributed to its embellishment ; the one by a temple of Siva, and the other by a Brahminical college. Besides this, Jayapira built Malhanapur in Kashmir, and his wives founded the cities Kalyanapur and Kamalapur, places named after themselves.

After a short period of tranquillity, Jayapira resumed his military enterprises. His first exploit was the reduction of a strong fort belonging to Bhimasena, king of the eastern region, and he thence proceeded against Aramuri, the magician king of Nepal,[26] whom, at the end of two or three days' march, he found posted with his forces on the southern bank of a river. The appearance of the enemy inflamed the courage of the king to temerity. Without a previous knowledge of the country, he rushed into the river, and left his bravest warriors behind him. The stream at first was no more than knee deep, but it suddenly rose, and swept away the king and his army. The greater part of the soldiers were drowned. The king, continuing to struggle with the waves, was carried down the stream. The cries of one army were echoed by the shouts of the other and some soldiers of the enemy mounted on inflated skins, rushed into the torrent, and captured the drowning prince. He was dragged to the shore, and confined in a strong castle on

[25] It is not practicable to ascertain with any degree of certainty any further particulars relating to the individuals named in the text. Bhatta is a title rather than a name, and is applied to several authors known to be natives of Kashmir, as Mammata Bhatta, the author of the *Kavya Prakasa*, and others. Damodara may be the author of the musical work called *Sangita Damodara* and there is a Vamana Acharya, who is the author of a set of poetical *Sutras* and of a *Vritti* or gloss upon them. The poetical propensities of the prince accord with the character of these writings. The other names offer nothing even for conjecture.

[26] There is no such name however in Kirkpatrick's lists of the Nepal kings.

the banks of the Gandika,[27] his broken and dismayed army retreating hastily to Kashmir.

The return of the troops, carrying the news of their discomfiture, and of the captivity of the king, spread consternation throughout Kashmir. The ministers immediately assembled to deliberate on what was to be done, when Deva Sarma, the son of the faithful Mitra Sarma, undertook to effect the liberation of the monarch. For this purpose he wrote to Aramuri, holding out promises of securing to him both the kingdom and treasures of Jayapira, if admitted to his presence. The terms were readily accepted, and the minister attended by a considerable body of forces, entered Nepal. His army he led to the banks of the Gandika, opposite to the fort which held his master captive, whilst he himself repaired to the court of Aramuri. At a private conference with the king of Nepal, Deva Sarma represented to him that the treasures of Jayapira were with the army, but their amount and distribution were known to Jayapira alone; that it would be advisable therefore for him to have an interview with that prince, and learn from him under some plausible pretence, these particulars, as otherwise the money might be lost or embezzled, and Aramuri be disappointed of a valuable prize. The Nepalese was deceived. Orders were given for Deva Sarma to be admitted privately to Jayapira, and the minister thus found himself in his master's presence.

In the interview that followed, Deva Sarma urged the king to let himself down from the window of his prison, and swim over the river to his troops, but Jayapira urged its impracticability, not only on account of the height of the window from the ground, but the impossibility of crossing the torrent without assistance. After some discussion, the minister withdrew, purposing professedly to return, but as a considerable interval elapsed during which he did not appear, the king went to seek him, and found him dead on the floor of an adjoining chamber, strangled with his own turban. Beside him lay a leaf, on which he had written these words with his nail; "You must effect your escape; I die to enable you; my body inflated with your breath will serve you as a float, tie yourself with my turban, quickly cross the river." Penetrated with admiration at the proof of attachment, and with grief for the loss of so faithful a friend.

27 Possibly the Gandaki or Gandak river. If however the fort of Bhimsena should be Bima near Nagrakot, this appellation must be applied to some other river.

the king obeyed his posthumous counsel, and safely effected a junction with his troops. Eager to wipe off his disgrace he fell upon the unprepared and astonished Nepalese, killed their king and left their country a depopulated waste.

Returning to Kashmir Jayapira spent some time in the enjoyment of the treasures he had acquired by the late expedition, when an extraordinary occurrence gave a new complexion to his character, and changed him into an oppressive and extortionary prince. Mahapadma the Naga appeared to him in a dream and implored his aid against a magician of the Naga and carry him off. Mahapadma promised the king as a reward for his protection, that he would reveal to him the existence of a gold mine, and then disappeared. In the morning, the king not quite satisfied of the veracity of the Naga, sent for the magician, and desired him to show him the person of the snake God. This the magician effected ; the waters of a lake retiring at his command, exposed the Naga and his serpent train. Jayapira however would not allow the magician to seize his prey, but ordering him to recall the waters of the lake, gave him a liberal recompense, and sent him to his own country. The Naga soon visited him again in his slumbers, but instead of gold, he punished him for his want of faith, by discovering to him the site of a copper mine, a source of considerable though inferior wealth. The mine was accordingly wrought, and in the course of his reign the king coined 100 crores of Dinars[28] less one, challenging all prices of the world to exceed this coinage, and complete the 100-crore.

The taste for wealth acquired by the king became fatal to his subjects. To accumulate treasure he levied heavy exactions on all ranks of people, and particularly oppressed the brahmans, by resuming the endowments, which he or his predecessors had bestowed upon them. Their complaints and remonstrances were unavailing with the king and his ministers, Siva Dasa and others, a set of Kayasthas, incapable of any generous feelings, whose extortion drove a hundred brahmans of Tulamula to drown themselves in the Chandrabhaga. To the supplications of the sacerdotal order, the king showing entire indifference, he at last attracted their menaces. These he ridiculed, but was finally punished for his impiety. In consequence of a curse denounced upon him by one of the order, he met with an accidental fall. A wound ensued in one of his legs, and this

[28] These were copper Dinars it is to be supposed.

breeding a number of worms, which preyed upon the king's body, he died in the greatest agony, after a reign of thirty-one years.[29] Lalitapira, who succeeded Jayapira was his son, by Durga Devi. He was a dissolute prince, who lavished his father's ill-gotten treasures on parasites and prostitutes, and instead of pandits and heroes, made buffoons and catamites his companions. He died after a reign of twelve years, of the grossest and lowest debauchery.

Sangramapira, his brother by another mother, the princess Kalyàna Devi, next ascended the throne. He was also known by the name of Prithivyapira : He reigned seven years.[30] The

[29] The fate of this prince, as told with great exultation in the original, is a curious specimen of Brahminical arrogance and superstition. It is not without a parallel however in the writers of Europe during the ascendancy of monkish authority. The conversation between the prince and priests, narrated in a somewhat dramatic form, is not without spirit. We may easily put it into dialogue.

A Brahman. Manu, Mandhata, Rama, and other sovereigns, mighty as they were, treated with reverence and awe the Brahmanical order, whose resistless wrath consumes earth and its mountains, hell and its serpent brood, and even Swarga and its gods, and king.

The King. Here's a big mouth, that fed upon a beggar's crumbs and drunk with pride, talks of its power with all the confidence of a holy seer.

Ittila, a Brahman. The revolutions of time have worked some change, but it is by submitting to a master, that we have ceased to be Rishis.

The King. Who art; thou? Viswamitra perhaps, or Vasishtha, or Agastya? I crave your pardon.

Ittila. And thou—thou art Harischandra, Trisanku or Nahusha. If so, I am Viswamitra, or who I please.

The King. By the anger of Viswamitra, Harishchandra was destroyed; what am I to dread from your mighty indignation ?

Ittila. (Rubbing his hand on the ground) Lord of all time, at my just indignation, let the punishment due to the insulter of a Brahman fall upon this prince.

The King : Let it fall; why does it delay? (The King's golden staff slips and he tumbles.)

The Brahman. Ha ! Babbler, has it not fallen on thee!!

[30] My manuscript has seven; Abul fazl has thirty-seven; which is an evident error as is shown by the aggregate of the reigns of the Dynasty which he calls 257 years, 5 months and 20 days but which according to the addition of several dates is 287—5. There being just the thirty years too much; the names in the translated *Ain-i-Akbari* here are written successively, Laltanand, Sangramanand, Brispat.

next monarch of Kashmir was Chippatajaya, a son of Lalitapira, by a prostitute, named Jaya Devi, otherwise Kalyapali, as the daughter of a Kalyapala or distiller, of Acha village. The brothers of this woman had been brought to court by the king, and their nephew, being yet a minor, they took the government into their own hands. They were five in number, named Padma, Utpala, Kalyana, Mamma, and Dharma, and their ambition opens a scene of domestic discord and calamity to which we have yet been strangers in the history of Kashmir.

The uncles of the young king divided amongst themselves the places and profit of the government, and assumed the supreme authority in the kingdom. The power they thus enjoyed they were not disposed to relinquish, and when the young prince exhibited a disposition to assert his independence, they deposed and put him to death, having suffered him to enjoy a nominal reign of twelve years. As they were too jealous of each other to suffer the ascendancy of either, they found it expedient to raise another prince to the throne, and they elevated to the titular rank of king, Tribhuvanapira, also called Ajitapira,[31] the grandson of Lalitaditya, and son of an elder brother of the last monarch. Under the name of Ajitapira, the five usurpers continued for a period of thirty-six years,[32] to possess the real sovereignty of Kashmir, and they veiled their violence and injustice by a liberal distribution of the public treasures, and the foundation of splendid temples, and rich endowments. It was not likely that the brothers should always continue on friendly terms, and a dispute arose between Mamma and Utpala, which occasioned a furious battle[33] on the borders of the Vitasta. Utpala, it should seem, was defeated and killed, chiefly through the valour of Yasovarma, the son of Mamma. The victor proceeded to dethrone and kill the king, his accession

[31] Ajayanand—*Ain-i-Akbari*.

[32] Reckoning, says our author, from the death of their nephew which happened in the year 89, startling us at once with a new computation, familiar of course to the Kashmirians, but to others requiring an explanation, which he has not given of it; the kind of date frequently recurs, and it is observable that it always stops short of 100, as if a cycle of 100 years had been adopted in Kashmir. Sometimes, as in the present instance, the date nearly corresponds with the odd years of the centuries of the Hijra, but the approximation is not always near enough to make it probable that reference to the Hijra is intended.

[33] It has been narrated, according to Kalhana, by Sankaka, a poet, in a poem named *Bhuvanabhyudaya*.

having been principally the work of Utpala, and place Anangapira,[34] a son of Sangramapira, on the throne.

The principal actors in the turbulent period of the last reign, now disappear from the history, and are succeeded by their sons, without our being informed further of the fortunes of the usurping fraternity. The princes became mere pegeants in the hands of these enterprising chiefs, with the unenviable distinction of being the first victims to the resentment of the conquerors. Ajitapira, we have seen, was put to death by the son of Mamma; his successor was not more fortunate; as after a short reign of three years, he suffered a similar fate from Sucha Varma, the now triumphant son of Utpala. This chief, created king, the son of Ajitapira, the predecessor of the last monarch: his name was Utpalapira,[35] and he was to be the last of the Karkota dynasty, for Sucha Varma being slain by a kinsman, his friends and followers, determined to place his son, Avanti Varma on the throne. Utpalapira was accordingly deposed and the son of Sucha Varma, the founder of the Utpala[36] dynasty, succeeded.

[34] Anankanand—*Ain-i-Akbari*

[35] Atbalanand.—*Ibid.*

[36] His grand-father: it is difficult here to keep the narrative clear, amidst the rapid succession of so many uncommon names. The deposition of Utpalapira happened, according to the author of the *Wakiat-i-Kashmir*, in the year of the Hijra 209. He is not quite right in his computation, as agreeably to our author's series of dates, it must be placed about A. D. 862. It may be here observed that Abul fazl has altered what may be called the family designation of most of the Karkota princes, and has changed the terminating name Apira to Ananda. In the next lists we have another change but this is a mere misreading, the family name *Varma* is converted into *Darma* the *Vau*, and *Dal*, being easily mistaken for each other. Varma is an adjunct expressing a Kshatriya or military descent. The present possessors however seem to have assumed it, as the founder of the family, Utpala, and his brothers were apparently of a less respectable origin.

CHAPTER III

A. D. 876. The accession of Avanti Varma[1] was not suffered to take place without opposition, and he had to undergo many conflicts with his own cousins, and even with his brothers, before his dominion was established. By his valour and prudence, however, aided by the sage counsel of Sura the minister, to whom he was chiefly indebted for his crown, he overcame all opposition, and remained the undisputed sovereign of Kashmir.

Having restored order and tranquillity, the king nominated Sura Varma his brother by a different mother, Yuvaraja, and the two brothers were both distinguished for their liberal and public spirit. The king gave large presents to the Brahmans, and the Yuvaraja bestowed upon them the Agraharas, K'haduya and Hastikarna, constructing a temple and statue of Gokula. Their example was followed by the younger brothers, and the ministers of the two princes, and variety of towns, temples and images embellished the kingdom. Amongst these we may specify the following : Avantipura, a city founded by the king at Viswakeswara Kshetra, in which he also erected a temple to Avantiswar or Siva, whose worship he had now adopted, in place of the Vaishnava tenets in which he had been educated. He also erected here three statues of the same deity, under the names of Tripureswara, Bhutesa and Vijayesa, with bathing vessels and stools of silver.

Surapur, a city founded by the minister; also a temple of the associated Sivas, and a college for ascetics at Sureswari-khetra. His son also established a *Matha* and his wife built the temple of Sada Siva at Surapur, a city which has since changed its name to Dhacca.[2]

The Minister who was thus the founder of cities, was also a munificent patron of the learned and the names of Muktakana,

[1] Aduntderma.—Abul fazl.

[2] Not the modern Dhacca of course. There is a place so called in Kashmir upon the Jhelum, south-west of Bijore. At present indeed it is scarcely within the limits of the province, and must be comprised in the states, said in Elphinstone's map, to be subject to independent Rajas, immediately south of Kashmir.

Siva Swami, Ananda Vardhana, Ratnakana, and Ramaja are enumerated as illustrious objects of his patronage.[3]

The reign of Avanti Varma was rendered remarkable by a severe famine, occasioned it is said by the rivers deserting their customary beds and submerging from time to time whole villages. The dearth was so excessive that many perished, amongst whom were Kallatta Bhatta and other eminent men. A *Khari*[4] of grain sold for a thousand and fifty dinars.

This impoverished state of the country continued for ten years, till Sujjya remedied the evil. The birth of this person was regarded as mysterious. He was found exposed in an earthen vessel by a *Chandali*, by whom he was suckled and brought up. Hearing the causes of the irregular swelling of the river discussed, he expressed his conviction that he could apply a remedy, and his words having been reported to the king, he was brought before Avanti Varma. The mode he proposed to adopt he declined explaining, and he was looked upon by the ministers as an idiot or a cheat. The king notwithstanding determined to give him a trial, and allowed him at his request to take from the treasury several bags of Dinars. With these in his possession, Sujjya retired to the site of a village named Anandaka, where, getting into a boat, he advanced into the water; when in the centre of the pool he threw into it a bag of Dinars, and he repeated this wherever the water was collected. The villagers tempted by the hope of obtaining the money, combined to effect its recovery. They first blocked up with large stones, the channel of the Vitasta where it issues from the mountains, the banks being there contiguous. They then drained the country of the accumulated water, by cleaning the canals and outlets, through which it was accustomed to run ; the passages being cleared by this contrivance, the dyke was broken down, and the Vitasta rushing forth with an impetus, proportioned to the obstruction it had encountered for several days, hurried away every obstacle, and flowed in a rapid and fertilising torrent through its old, and through many new channels, to its junction with the Sindhu.[5] These two streams formerly met near the

[3] They are names however not known.

[4] The *Khari* is equal to two bushels, two pecks, one gallon and two thirds (*Asiatic Researches* V. 98) or about the third of a quarter. The Dinars, it may be suspected, were of copper.

[5] This cannot be the Indus, but must be the Sind river, which has its source in great Tibet.—*Ain-i-Akbari*, Vol. ii. pp. 158. It is not improbably a branch however of the Indus.

temple of Vainya Swami, but they now unite, observes our author, between that place and Vishnuswami or the towns of Parihasapura and Phalapura[6] and he adds, that some old trees existed in his time, bearing the marks of the ropes which the Nishadas,[7] had fastened there. Having collected massive stones to confine the Vitasta, Sujjya constructed the Mahapadma Saras, springing from which receptacle, the Vitasta darts forward with the rapidity of an arrow from a bow.[8]

Sujjya was not contented with remedying the evil ; he also provided against its recurrence, by the construction of dykes and canals, by which without fear of a deluge, the waters were distributed equally and plentifully to all parts of the kingdom. Such was the beneficial result of his measures, that a *Khari* of grain, which before the late dearth sold for 200 Dinars, has ever since been restricted to no more than thirty-six.[9] Sujjya was bountifully rewarded for his labours, and was enabled to perpetuate his name by founding Sujjyapur on the banks of the Vitasta, where it issues from the reservoir.

After enabling the ingenuity of Sujjaya to execute the beneficial arrangements above described, and witnessing the improving condition of his kingdom, Avanti Varma being taken ill, determined to end his days at Tripura Kshetra, and accordingly proceeded thither, where he resumed the Vaishnava faith, and listening to the perusal of the *Bhagavad Gita*, he terminated his career in the year 59, after a reign of 28 years and 3 months.

A. D. 905. As Avanti Varma was not succeeded by his

[6] The last must be Shahabadinpura where the Behut and Sind unite their streams.—*Ain-i-Akbari*, Vol. ii, p. 158.

[7] The low castes of villagers, he means, it may be supposed, and the ropes may have been part of a *Jhula* or swinging bridge.

[8] This should be the reservoir or bason at Vira Nag noticed by Forster, Vol. ii. p. 4, and according to the report which he repeats, constructed by Jahangir. This is an evident error however, as the same bason is thus mentioned by Abul fazl : "At Weersir is the source of the river Behut, with a bason measuring a *jareeb*, whence the water rushes out with an astonishing noise. The spring is called Wirnag. It has a stone border and on the east side are temples."—*Ain-i-Akbari*, Vol. ii. p. 155.

[9] This confirms what I have hinted that these *Dinars* were copper. The *Khari* is probably Abul fazl's *Kherwar* in which he says everything is estimated in Kashmir. The average price of this, ascertained when fixing the revenue of the province, turned out to be twenty-nine dams or pice. —*Ain-i-Akbari*. Vol. ii. p. 161.

brother, and not only a new king, but a new *Yuvaraja* was appointed upon his death, we are left to conclude, either that Sura Varma was dead or the office of *Yuvaraja* conferred no title to the succession, and was held at pleasure. It appears too, that at this time the great officers of the state continued to exercise the authoritative interference they had obtained under the last dynasty, and disposed at will of the functions of royalty. It is said accordingly that the son of Avanti Varma, Sankara Varma[10] was made king, by the power of the chamberlain Ratnavardhana, whilst Karnapa, sprung from one of the late king's brothers, procured the nomination of Sucha Varma, the son of Sura Varma, to succeed his father in the *Yauvarajya,* in opposition to the chamberlain and the king, a circumstance which led to a civil war between the superior and subordinate princes. In the contest many distinguished chieftains were slain, as Siva Sakti and others, but the king, with the aid of Samara Varma, and other leaders of note, finally prevailed, and established his authority in the kingdom.

Having thus secured himself at home, he directed his views to foreign conquest, and being joined by the king of Darvabhisara and other princes, he led into the plains an army said to consist of nine lakhs of foot, one of horse, and three hundred elephants. He first subdued Prithivi Chandra king of Traigarta,[11] who having left his son in his capital, advanced to do him homage, but upon beholding the immense host collected by the king, he was alarmed for his personal safety, and suddenly made his escape. Sankara Varma then rooted up the power of Alakhana[12] king of Gurjara, seizing his treasures, and kingdom, and leaving him only Tacca Desa. He entirely subverted the universal supremacy which had been seized by Bhoja[13] and made himself formidable to his neighbours on either side of him, the kings of Darat and Turushka[14] placed

[10] Sunkerderma.—Abul fazl.

[11] Part of Lahore.

[12] This is a strange name; it should be that of a Musalman but the Musalman princes could not have been then established in Gujarat. There is however a Gujarat in the Punjab, to which the Mahammadans were beginning to extend themselves, and which may be the state intended.

[13] Not in his life time it may be supposed, but Sankara Varma flourished about half a century earlier than has hitherto been assigned as Bhoja's date.

[14] We still have the Dards north-west of Kashmir; the Turushkas

between them like Aryavarta between the Himalaya and Vindya mountains. On his return to Kashmir he founded in Panchasatra, a city named after himself. It was constructed chiefly of materials furnished by the ruins of Parihasapura, and was distinguished by a temple dedicated to Siva as Śankara Gaurisa, and Sugandhesa, the latter named after the queen Sugandha, the daughter of the king of the North.

The disposition of Sankara Varma to accumulate wealth, degenerated into the most insatiable avarice, and subjected his people to every kind of extortion. He levied heavy tolls and taxes, exacted undue proportions of the produce of land, and let out to farm those lands which were the property of temples. He cheated his cultivators in the weight of the seed corn, and expected a full return, and he seems to have established a monopoly of sandal, incense, oil and many other articles of trade. His chief instruments in these oppressions were the Kayasthas, and especially one named Lavata, who received from the king a stipend of 3,000 Dinars, whilst Bhallata and other eminent poets about the court were kept without any pay. The chief minister represented the harshness of his commands in vain to the monarch. To his son who had expatiated to him on the afflictions of his people, he replied by desiring him to wait till he was king, when he might, if he pleased, relieve them, and he was equally insensible to the lesson he might have learnt from the neighbouring country of Darvabhisara, the king of which, with all his sons, had been lately killed in a popular commotion, occasioned by his oppressive government.

Sankara Varma possibly thought he should divert the attention of his subjects to less unpopular occurrences, by engaging them in military expeditions; for he is said now to have led an army to the north,[15] where he subdued the people along the Indus,[16] and entered the Urasa country, where he was

should be therefore to the south-east, and they were the Ghiznian Governors, probably, then dependent on the Samanian princes of Bokhara. The simile is applicable to such a position.

[15] Bedia-ud-din says, against Muhammadans of Khorasan; the followers of Islam having according to him spread their empire even to the Punjab in the preceding reign.

[16] The Sindhu, here the large river, as the other or smaller was already in his possession. The invasion took place into little Tibet, but the invaders could not have proceeded far, as they reached on their return

shot in the neck with an arrow by a mountaineer. He was immediately put into a litter, and his death, which took place shortly afterwards, concealed from the troops, who were immediately marched back to Kashmir with all possible expedition. They reached Holyasaka, a place on the frontier, in six days, where, being now out of danger, they halted to perform the funeral obsequies of the monarch. He was consumed on a stately pile; three of his queens, a pandit, named Jaya Sinha, and two of his servants, burning themselves with the body.[17]

A. D. 923. The son and successor of the last king, Gopala Varma being yet an infant, was placed under the tutelage of his mother Sugandha; she became regent during his minority, and her ascendancy involved the country in a series of intestine disorders, as she seems to have been a woman of a weak, if not vicious character; the minister and chief treasurer Prabhakara Deva was her favourite, and engrossed the whole power of the state. This man made Kamalaka, also named Sahi, Governor of Bhandapur, but he proving disobedient, it was taken from him, not without a conflict apparently and given to Toramana, the son of Lalita.

The reign of Gopal Varma was short; he was carried off by magical incantations, it is said, by the contrivance apparently of Prabhakara Deva, who was afraid of being called to account

the frontiers of Kashmir in six days. Who the Aurasas, the people of Urasa, were, is not easily conjectured; they could scarcely have been the Russians, called in the east Urus, whose power at this period, was first making its appearance in a different direction, and it is only in the absence of more satisfactory illustration, that I venture to suggest a connexion, between this word and the Ooloos, the hordes of the Tatars, and clans of the Afghans. The derivative name, applied to the people, is in favour of the conjecture, as it means children, whom the Hindus consider legitimate, being born of a man and woman of the same caste or tribe.

[17] These accompaniments of his cremation find an analogy in many parts of the south of India, as noticed by early travellers; they are not however directed by the Sastras, any more than the self-immolation on account of sorrow or sickness, of which we have several instances; the latter indeed in the present age is prohibited at any place except Prayaga. Several instances of suicide occur in the Hindu books, as Bhishma in the *Mahabharata*, and the father and the mother of the young ascetic killed accidently by Dasaratha, who mounted the funeral pile with their son, as told in the *Raghuvansa*, see *Asiatic Researches* Vol. x. These cases however are referred to former periods.

for the great deficiencies in the public treasury, which were ascribable to his own peculations. Rama Deva, the person employed by him, afterwards confessed the fact, and as the minister disappears from the history, we may suppose he paid the penalty of his crime. Sugandha, in the midst of her faults, appearing to entertain no ambitious views for herself, and to have cherished the memory of her son.

A brother of Gopala Varma succeeded him, but he expired after the short term of ten days, and as with him the race of Sankara Varma ended, the kingdom was now without a legal occupant. Sugandha seated herself on the throne, but either at her own desire, or compelled by the military leaders of the kingdom, she soon made way for another prince.

In this stage of Kashmirian history we are introduced rather abruptly to some new actors in the scene, who continued for a long period to influence very materially the disposal of the crown. They are of a military character evidently. It is only doubtful whether they are part of the native forces or whether they were mercenary bands of foreign adventurers. They are denominated Tatris and Ekangas, and it is perhaps not straining probability overmuch to conjecture that our author intends these words to represent what we should write Tatras and Afghans, men, who at all times have sold their services to the princes of India, and have not infrequently become the masters of those whom they originally obeyed.[18]

[18] The word Tatar for Tatri is an obvious conjecture. Ekanga for Afghan is not so satisfactory. *Eka* means one, and *Anga* limb or body figuratively as well as literally, and *Ekanga* may refer to some peculiarity of discipline, as to troops, fighting in a body. The origin of the word Afghan, says Elphinstone, is entirely uncertain, but it is probably modern. It is known to the Afghans themselves only through the medium of the Persian language. It has no meaning however in Persian, and they therefore probably borrowed it from some other quarter transmitting it in their ordinary manner. There is some probability therefore about the etymology suggested. The Afghans it is asserted inhabited the mountains of Ghor at a very remote period, and seem to have been established in the north eastern mountains of Afghanistan in the ninth century, (Elphinstone's *Cabul*, p. 157.), expelling thence, probably about that time the Damaras, who from our history appear to have occupied, till the ninth century, that part of the vicinity of Kashmir. The mercenary character of the Tatris is repeatedly alluded to. They are said to have been attracted in the country by the Hundikas of the king of Kanouj, and they are compared in one place to prostitues who saw no merit in a man but his money.

Whatever may have been her inducements, Sugandha, after holding the reins of government for two years, recommended to the ministers and officers to choose as king Nirjita Varma the grand-son of Sura Varma. It was objected to him however that he was a cripple, and therefore not fit to rule, but as his family descent was highly respectable, the chiefs determined to nominate his son, and Partha[19] was accordingly crowned king of Kashmir.

At the end of ten years, the leaders of the Ekangas dissatisfied with the prince, and jealous of the greater share which the Tatri foot had in his nomination, determined to replace Sugandha in the government; they accordingly proceeded to her residence at Hushkapur, and placing her at their head returned to the capital. They were met by the Tatris in the pay of the king, and after a severe conflict were totally routed. The queen was taken prisoner and put to death at Nishpalakaluhar.

The victorious troops now considered the kingdom at their disposal and yielded reluctant obedience to their prince for a further period of five years. At last their insubordination broke out with ungovernable force, and their avarice, which was insatiable, led them to accept the offers of the father of Partha and to place the cripple on the throne. The revolution was facilitated by a period of general distress, occasioned by a famine, consequent upon the unseasonable inclemency of the weather.

The reign of this prince lasted but one year. His throne and life were assailed by various enemies. His son Partha was endeavouring to recover his supremacy. His ministers Sankara Vardhana and Sugandhaditya were plotting for their own accession, and his queen was enagged in a criminal intercourse with the latter, and prepared to commit any atrocity to secure the undisturbed gratification of her libidinuous passion. It is not at all extraordinary therefore, that he should have been crowned one year and deposed and slain the next.

A. D. 942. C. Y. 97. The successor of the cripple was an infant son, named Chakra Varma who under the protection of his maternal grand-father, enjoyed the sovereignty ten years; at the expiration of this time however, the sons of Meru Vardhana, the elder of whom Sankara Vardhana, was minister to the late king, set up another of his sons, Sura Varma, and expelled the reigning prince. A most turbulent period now

[19] Bareth—*Ain-i-Akbari.*

ensues, and the several princes rise and fall, sometimes repeatedly, in rapid succession.

A. D. 953-9. C. Y. 7. Sura Varma, after a nominal reign of one year, was deposed by the discontented Tatri troops, and Partha again crowned king. He soon made way for Chakra Varma, once more, whose bribes had won these venal soldiers to his interest. Unable however to satisfy their repeated demands, he was obliged to abdicate, and seek safety in flight, whilst Sankara Vardhana endeavoured to effect a purchase of the crown from the mercenary troops; in this he was foiled; his ambassador to them, his own brother Sambhu Vardhana, making the bargain for himself, and being elevated by them to the throne, a measure however that appears to have contributed to check, if it did not annihilate the power, of the pretorian Tatris.

Chakra Varma in his flight had found an asylum near Dhacca,[20] at the house of a Damara, and one it may be presumed who was possessed of powerful influence with the mountain tribes. Induced by the liberal promises of the king, and his reiterated assurances of eternal gratitude, he collected a considerable number of his countrymen, and advanced with Chakra Varma once more towards the capital.

The entrance of the king into Srinagar was effected without opposition; indignant at the fraud practised on him by his brother, Sankara Vardhana had assembled an army, and advanced from Maruwa,[21] where he was stationed at the period of his negotiation for the crown. To maintain the kingdom, Sambhu Vardhana had marched to oppose him with the troops in his interest, and the capital of Kashmir, being thus left without defenders, fell an easy prey to the invader. The approach of Chakra Varma appears to have reunited the two brothers, as we find them both present in a furious conflict fought near Padmapur between their forces, and the Damaras under Chakra Varma, in which the latter obtained a most decisive victory. Five or six thousand of the Tatris were slain. Sankara Vardhana graced the bed of heroes and Sambhu Vardhana attempting to reassemble the scattered fugitives of his army, was shortly afterwards taken prisoner and put to death.

[20] See the note on Surapur, the city itself must have been in the quarter of Kashmir peopled by the Damaras.

[21] Any dry or desert soil, of which we have several extensive tracts to the south-west of Kashmir.

The power of the Tatris appears to have been completely broken by their defeat, as although mention of them does recur in the course of the history, no important part in the revolutions of the crown is henceforward assigned to them.

Chakra Varma returned to the capital in triumph. Mounted on a superb charger, in the centre of his victorious cavalry, holding in his left hand his helmet, and touching his turban in courtesy to the crowd with his right, he entered the city, amidst the clamour of kettle-drums and the shouts of the multitude. He soon however forfeited his popularity; being fascinated by the attractions of two daughters of a Dombha,[22] who, as public singers appeared before the king, he took them into his harem, and devoted his whole time to their impure society. The constquences were obvious : he incurred the reprehension of the wise and respectable, and what was of more importance to him, by promoting the low connexions of his favourites, above his former ministers of the military and sacerdotal orders, he roused their indignation and resentment.

Amongst those who felt aggrieved by the preference thus shown to an out-caste tribe, the Damaras were particularly distinguished. They who had been the chief instruments of the king's triumph, were now neglected with the rest of his adherents, and compelled to make way for those, whose birth and services gave them no claim to pre-eminence. They felt the neglect of the king the more severely, as contrasted with his past assurances of favour, and they determined to make him suffer the effects of their vindictive spirit. A party of them accordingly contrived to gain by night, admission into the palace, and falling upon the king, in the apartment of his favourite mistress, unarmed and unprepared, they easily sacrified him to their fury. He was slain after a reign of nearly fourteen years, interrupted from time to time by the temporary rule of his occasionally successful competitors.

Unamatti Varti, a son of Pártha, was now placed upon the throne, in preference to his father, who was still alive. His claims to this election cannot be easily conceived, especially as in the grovelling tastes of this prince as well as in ferocity of temper, he exceeded all who reigned before or after his time. His associates were dancers, singers and buffoons ; his favourite pastime, fighting birds or beasts, in which Parva Gupta by his

[22] A man of the lowest class, by whom all impure offices are performed.

superior skill, was his principal minister and friend, notwithstanding which he engaged in treasonable designs, aided by Bhubhatta, Sarvata, Saja, Kumuda and Amritakara. These individuals divided amongst themselves the chief offices of profit and power whilst Rakshasa, a Damara, commanded the army. By the advice of these miscreants, and the suggestion of his own sanguinary disposition, the king commanded a general slaughter to be made of all whom he thought he had occasion to hate or fear, and did not spare the members of his own family. His brothers he shut up in a dungeon, and starved to death, and his own father was dragged from his retirement and murdered by order of this unnatural son. His barbarity did not stop there; he went to view his father's corpse, and made the murderers show the wounds, that each had inflicted. They hesitated to do this in the king's presence, when Parva Gupta, to reprove the backwardness of one of them, his own son, Deva Gupta, struck his dagger into the lifeless body, to the great mirth and satisfaction, it is said, of the king. In further proof of this prince's atrocious character it is related that upon its becoming necessary to oppose Damaras, who pillaged the country with impunity, the king used to amuse himself with cutting off the heads of his attendants and subjects and the breasts of the women, in order to try the temper of his sword, and perfect himself, he said, in the use of his weapons. Death put a stop to his ferocious practices, and released Kashmir from his tyranny, after it had endured it a little more than two years.

The son of the parricide, Sura Varma[23] succeeded him. He was yet an infant, under the management of his mother, and his nominal reign was of short duration. Kamala Vardhana, who had been employed to clear the country of the Damaras, had succeeded in the undertaking, and had made peace and alliance with the chiefs of Kampana and Marawa. He now returned accompained by all the leaders, and the Tatris and Ekangas, and displayed all the pomp of royalty, although he had not assumed the name of king. Doubtful of his purpose, and deserted by all her late adherents, the queen fled with her infant, unattended, into the forests.

Kamala Vardhana although now in possession of the military power, and consequently of the kingdom, hesitated to mount the throne, a piece of folly our author observes, only ascribable to the treacherous counsels of unfaithful ministers

[23] Abul fazl confounds this with the former prince of the same name.

or to the adumbration of his intellect, as a punishment of evil done in a former life. His moderation did not proceed from indifference to royalty, as he collected the brahmans, and desiring them to nominate a king, attempted to win them over to his interests. The opportunity was lost. The brahmans desirous of selecting a suitable person, or instigated by other motives, deliberated for some time about the choice, and despatched emissaries to ascertain the merits and claims of various candidates.

Amongst others, the widow of Unmatti Varti sent messengers to the brahmans to solicit their support of her son. On their road, they were encountered by a youth, who was just returning to his own country, and who accompanied them to the capital, where the brahmans, unable to resist what our author thinks the impulse of destiny, proclaimed him, as soon as they beheld him, sovereign of Kashmir.

The person thus suddenly elevated to the throne was Yasaskara Deva. He was the son of Kama Deva, born of Vira Deva, an inhabitant of the village of Pisachapur. Kama Deva in his youth had been brought up by Meru Vardhana, and being a lad of abilities, rose with the patronage of that minister to the Ganjadhicharya, the command of the guards, which he held under the reign of Sankara Varma. Having occasion to dread the hostility of Prabhakar, the favourite of Sugandha, he determinded to place his son out of danger, and sent him into another country with a young friend named Phalguna. They had resided abroad for some time. At length his father being dead, and propitious dreams exciting his hopes, Yasaskara resolved to return to his native country, and it was upon this occasion that he encountered the agents of the queen, and learning from them the object of their journey, accompanied them to the capital, where he so unaccountably gained the unsolicited choice of the sacerdotal electors.

A. D. 961. The vigour and equity of the new king fully justified his election. He re-established order and security, and gave to Kashmir a period of repose which had been long unknown. Theft and murder were abolished, the roads were perfectly safe, and the shops were left open throughout the night without a guard ; the distinction of classes was rigidly maintained, and the *Chandalas* no longer administered the affairs of state, nor did the Brahmans carry arms. We have several anecdotes of this king's acumen and jusice. One of them is narrated by Abul fazl, a reference to whom will perhaps be sufficient to satisfy any curiosity that may be excited on this head.

After promoting the happiness of his subjects for several years, Yasaskara, was doomed to suffer the loss of his own. One of his wives was detected in an intrigue with a watchman of the palace, a man of low caste, and it appears that the king was more afflicted by this latter circumstance, than anything else, as it had prophaned the purity of his birth. To expiate the stain thus contracted, he made liberal donations to the Brahmans, and founded a Matha, but continuing to dwell upon his disgrace, his health became affected, and he retired to the college of his own foundation to expire.

Before leaving the palace, the king directed the nobles and leaders to elect as his successor, his kinsman Varnata, the son of Rama Deva passing over his own son Sangrama Deva, of whose legitimacy he entertained some doubts. The arrangement thus made was far from agreeable to the men in power, for Varnata was a prince in the vigour of life, whilst Sangrama Deva was an infant, during whose feeble administration they flattered themselves that they should be able to appropriate the wealth and influence of the government to themselves and their adherents. By their intrigues, therefore, Varnata was thrown into prison, and although he appears to have escaped at the time, he shortly afterwards fell a victim to the jealousy and ambition of the strongest party, by whom Sangrama Deva was established in the government.

The old king lingered some time after he had made the fruitless disposition of the succession, but he was surrounded by the creatures of the intriguers, and there is reason to suppose that they accelerated his death by poison. Parva Gupta and his partizans had now obtained what was still but a secondary object of their ambition, and their past success encouraged them to elevate their views to royalty itself. The seasons befriended their designs, and the discontent of the people occasioned by the pressure of a general scarcity afforded them a ready instrument for effecting their purpose. An insurrection was speedily excited. A tumultuary mob, chiefly composed of the military and headed by Parvagupta and his confederates, attacked the palace. They slew Rama Vardhana, the chief minister, who had attempted in vain to defend it, and penetrated to the presence of the king. Seizing his person they bound him with fetters of flowers, dragged him to another apartment, and put him to death. After which, they tied a stone to his neck and threw the body into the Vitasta. Parvagupta, then in complete armour, and with his sword drawn, seated himself on the throne, and received the homage of his accomplices and of the terrified citizens. After a short reign at little more than a year, this prince suffered the fate due to his crimes. He was slain by a party of enemies at Sureswari Kshetra and left the crown to his son.

Kshemagupta was a prince of depraved habits, and spent his time in low and sensual indulgence. Wine and women occupied his whole attention, and profligate characters engrossed his company. It was not at all extraordinary therefore that the kingdom should become a prey to civil dissension and foreign inroad, as the affairs of state were entirely neglected, and the ministers alone fit to conduct them, were obliged to abandon the court in order to avoid the ridicule and abuse, or even personal contumely which they were compelled to receive from the prince and the companions of his revels. Consequently, besides private hostilities between Phalguna, and some of the king's friends, the ruler of Kampana engaging in a contest with the Damaras, burnt and destroyed the Vihara of Jayendra, and demilished a brass image of Sugata, and the king of the C'hasas compelled Kshemagupta to cede to him six and thirty villages, after burning many Viharas.[24]

The ruler of Lahore, Sinha Raja, now gave Kshemagupta in marriage his daughter Didda, the grand-daughter by the mother's side of Sahi, a princess destined to bear an important part in the subsequent revolutions of Kashmir. Her charms seem to have had little effect upon her husband, for after his marriage he adopted a new amusement, and devoted all his time to the pleasure of the chace. They were the occasion of his death, for having pursued a jackal for a considerable distance, and urged the beast to the pains of death, the prince observed flame issuing from the mouth of the animal as it expired; struck with alarm at this portent, he was instantly seized with a fit of trembling which terminated in the Lutamaya[25] fever, a fever that is invariably fatal. He was carried to Kshema Matha near Hush-Kapur, where he died after a reign of eight years and six months.

[24] These broils which are very obscurely and confusedly narrated in the original, were perhaps of a religious complexion, and may be connected with the persecution of the Buddhists of which so much is said and so little is known, by the Hindus.

[25] We have here two strange subjects; in the superstitious idea of flames issuing from the jackal's mouth, and the nature of the Lutamaya disease; the first is common; it is the current belief in India that any animal urged to death by a chace emits flames from his mouth before he expires.

Abhimanyu, the son of Kshemagupta, succeeded his father. At first his early age and afterwards his tranquil temper, left the reins of administration in the hands of his mother whose defective character was far from equal to the task and whose supremacy introduces us consequently to a scene of unprecedented tumult and disorder.

The queen's first impulse was to burn herself with her husband, from no better motive the Hindu writer admits, than the pride of birth, and fear of Phalguna, the late king's minister, and father-in-law, by another of the monarch's wives, and who on that account had always been hostile to Didda. She was also embarrassed at the outset of her career by a conflagration of a most alarming nature, which broke out at the fair of Tungimara and extended to Vitala Sutrapata, consuming an immense number of villages, and many large palaces and temples. This added to the dread of Phalguna, now all powerful, would certainly have given her a claim to the honours of a *Sati*, had she not been dissuaded from it by Nara Vahana, a man of great merit and fidelity, attached to her service. The return of one of the king's sons, Kardama, contributed also to the consolidation of her authority. He had been to the Ganges with the bones of Kshemagupta, attended by a select body of troops, and as he was no friend to the usurping Phalguna, that minister thought it politic to come to an accommodation with the queen, and upon the reconcilation taking place, he withdrew for a season from public affairs.

The next opponent of the regent's authority, and she appears to have encountered opposition in rapid succession, were Mahiman, and Patala, the sons of Suja and Bhubhatta, two of Parvagupta's friends and co-adjutors. These youths had been brought up in the palace, but jointly resenting some personal affronts offered by the queen regent to Mahiman, they plotted a conspiracy for his elavation to the throne. In this they were joined by sevaral of the leading men of Parihaspura and Lalitapura and succeeded in levying a respectable force, and leading it against the Rani Didda, with the assistance of Nara Vahana, prepared to engage them, but unwilling to trust the decision to the chance of war, she engaged by large presents, the Brahmans of Lalitapura to come forward as mediators. Their mediation was irresistible, and Mahiman and his confederates were compelled, although reluctantly, to abandon their design and submit to the forgiveness of the queen : a curious proof of the influence of the sacerdotal order in Kashmir in comparatively modern times.

One of the chief leaders of the late conspiracy was Yasodhara, to whom the queen gave the government of Kampana, to bind him more firmly to her interests. A war now arose between him and Sahi, governor or king of Dhacca, and the later was defeated, and compelled to pay tribute. Proud of his success, and instigated by evil counsellors, Yosadhara soon found cause of complaint against the regent, and led his army against her, supported by Nara-Vahana. The regent resolved to encounter him in the field, and a battle accordingly ensued, in which Yasadhara was defeated. He was taken prisoner, and thrown into confinement with all his family, whilst many of his adherents, also captives, were thrown into the Vitasta, with large stones fastened to their necks.

It would be useless to prosecute the story of civil discord further. The nobles and governors had in fact all become more or less independant of a monarchy, long feebly administered, and were ready on every slight pretext to lead their military followers to the field. By the counsels and conduct of Nara-Vahana, the regent uniformly triumphed and appears to have deserved the success she enjoyed; his death however was the ruin of her credit, if not of her power, and she appears hereafter in the character only of a cruel, libidinous and ambitious woman.

At this period Abhimanyu diéd, our author says, of consumption. Mohammed Azim asserts that he was poisoned by his mother. The former account, however, is most trustworthy, especially as corroborated by the sequel, which represents her as engaged for a year afterwards, in laying the foundations of cities, and pious and public edifices, in order to dispel her grief. In this way she is said to have founded Kankanapur and Diddapur Mathas, for the Saura and Lata Brahmans, and the temples of Abhimanyu Swami and Didda Swami, several Chatur Salas or Sarais and many Viharas, and to have made the conflux of the Sindhu and Vitasta a place of great sanctity. At the end of twelve months, however, her ambition revived, and upon reassuming the administration she thought it advisable to rid herself of her grandson Nandigupta, who had succeeded his father and whom she put to death.

Tribhuvana, another grandson, was next placed upon the throne, but speedily shared the fate of his brother, and a third named Bhimagupta was elevated to the dangerous distinction. Didda now chose a new favourite, and a *Chasa* named Tunga, originally a keeper of buffaloes, and subsequently a courier in the service of the minister, enjoyed her affection and favours. He soon acquired the ascendancy at court, and thrust himself and his five brothers into all the most important posts. The intrusion of this upstart race was warmly resented by the Kashmirian nobles, who called to their assistance Vigraha Vaga, a nephew of the queen's, and a man of high spirit and great power. Tunga was obliged to resign his newly acquired authority and preserved his life only by the interference of the Brahmans, whom the bribes of the queen had induced to intercede. Vigraha finding it impracticable therefore to afford that redress to the Kashmirians which they had solicited, retired to his own territory, and left the ascendancy to be recovered by the favourite of the queen, who notwithstanding his low origin, appears to have been a man of firmness and activity. The young prince Bhimagupta betraying, as he advanced in years, some indications of an independent spirit, was now removed from the throne, and privately put to death. Kardama Raja and several of the leading men suffered the same fate, and the Brahmans who had saved the life of Tunga were thrown by him into prison, probably to compel them to refund the reward of their late mediation. Seriusly alarmed for their safety, the nobles now called to their aid the Prince Prithivi Pala, who marched with his troops to their aid, and occupied the capital. Tunga, however, foiled his adversaries. Advancing upon the city with a large force, he set the suburbs on fire, and cutting off the retreat of the enemy effected the destruction of a great part of their army. Prithivi Pala[26] was compelled to submit to Tunga, and to purchase his safety by engaging to pay tribute to the sovereign of Kashmir.

The transaction thus described, is the last instance of civil dissension that seems to have occurred under the reign of Didda Rani. Triumphant over both foreign and domestic foes, she was now at leisure to regulate the succession to the kingdom, and

[26] The territory governed by this prince is not named. He might in fact have not yet been in possession of any, as the son only of the sovereign of Lahore, Anandapala, whose successor about the date of the above events, is named by Ferishta, Pitterugepal.—Dow. vol. i. p. 58. It must be observed however that if the dates of our history and the Muhamadan history accorded, we should have had in the former some notice of the repeated visits of Kashmir paid by Mahmud in 1005, 1015 and 1018; the history of Kalhana coming down to 1025; one or other however may err by a few years, if indeed the error is not as much of facts as of dates. The author of the *Tabaqat-i-Akbari* states indeed that Mahmoud was repeatedly foiled in his attempts to penetrate into Kashmir.

adopted Sangrama Deva, the son of her brother Udaya Raja, as her associate in the government, and as the future supreme ruler of Kashmir.

A. D. 1025. C. Y. 79. This was the last act of her life, and is the last event recorded by our author, whose history closes with the death of Didda Rani and accession of Sangrama Deva in the 79th year of the Kashmirian cycle, or the year of our Lord 1025, and after the queen had held the sole sovereignty of the country for three and twenty years.[27]

[27] It is not correct to say that Kalhana's History of Kashmir closes with the death of Didda Rani. His work comes down to 1148 A.D., and is continued by a series of other writers to the date of the conquest of Kashmir by Akbar in the 16th century. All the MSS. on kings of Kashmir were not available to Wilson when he wrote. It is an essay on an imperfect Sanskrit work to which he had access—a resume mixed up with facts gleaned from Mahommedan histories. For obvious reasons, we have not thought it advisable to make any textual addition or alteration. —Ed.

CHAPTER IV

REMARKS ON THE HISTORY AND CHRONOLOGY OF KASHMIR

Having now completed the sketch of Kashmirian history, it may be expected that we should revert to it for a moment, for the purpose of taking a concise view of the light which it reflects upon the general history and chronology of the Hindus. Objects of more interest than the local transactions which it details, and which, circumscribed within the narrow limits of a petty state, of remote site and difficult access, are neither in themselves, nor in their effects upon their neighbours, of any magnitude or importance. It may be added however that they are of the same general character, as the events which make up history in all countries, and may not be therefore devoid of interest, to the mind that can be contented to contemplate man, in so sequestered a region, as the valley of Kashmir.

It appears very evident that Kashmir has been a regular kingdom for a period that transcends the limits of legitimate history, and even if we feel disposed to contest the accounts of our author, and to dispute his series of Dynasties and Princes, we must still rest satisfied with the proof of its existence either under the names of Kaspapyras or Abisaras,[1] as early as the days of Herodotus and Alexander. There can be no doubt however of the regular organization of this state at a period, much antecedent, and it is probable that in remote times it exercised a more decided influence on the concerns of India, than it has done for many centuries past. It seems highly probable also that it was the original dominion of the Pandava princes and that it furnished in them sovereigns to the plains of Hindustan.

The religion of Kashmir has in like manner been Hindu from a very remote date. Originally no doubt it was the Ophite or snake worship, but this is a part of the Hindu ritual, and the Nagas are included in the orthodox pantheon. The adoration of Siva was soon engrafted upon this, even if the two rites were not originally identified.

[1] See Appendix No. VIII.

It appears that the Buddhist schism was known in Kashmir at a very early period, and possibly preceded the introduction of a fully organized Brahmanical priesthood. It probably in short preceded the introduction of the Brahmanical caste. Asoka, although a worshipper of Siva, is said to have countenanced this new faith. His son Jaloka commenced his reign with serious efforts to suppress it, and it was possibly partly with this view, that he introduced the colony of Brahmans from Kanouj. Towards the close of his reign however he relaxed in his hostility to the Buddhists, and his successor, although a pious worshipper of Siva, appears to have participated in the same feelings. The legend of Damodara's transformation indicates his having incurred the enmity of the Brahmanical order.

The period that immediately ensues, is of great interest in the religious history of India. Kashmir became a Buddhist country under Tartar princes, shortly after the death of Sakya Singha, according to our author, and he agrees nearly with the Chinese authorities, as to the period at which that legislator flourished, and according to them, in this very country. The latter seems to be an error; it may however indicate the direction where the birth of the elder Buddha happened, and in connexion with the circumstances narrated by the Sanskrit writer, seems to point out an extra-Indian origin for this religion.[2] Its predominance in Kashmir was of short duration, as although not extirpated, it speedily and finally gave way before the prepon-

[2] Sir William Jones alludes to the white and ruddy complexion of Buddha as calculated to convince Bailly of the Tartar origin of this legislator. Remusat (in the *Journal Des Savans*, Octre 1819) commenting on some of the epithets descriptive of Buddha, contained in a Polyglot Buddhist vocaulary complied in China (or rather translated from some Indian work, one of the languages being Sanskrit) notices this ephithet Suvarnachhavi, the golden hued, but without being inclined to draw such a conclusion from it as Bailly might have drawn. The description of this Buddha however, as contained in the Vocabulary described by Remusat, *Mines de L'Orient*, vol. iv. connected with the circumstances we have had occasion to notice in the text, tends very much to confirm the idea of the original Buddhist schism having been imported from Tartary. The name of this legislator, Sakya, is further evidence to the same effect; its Sanskrit etymologies are very unsatisfactory, and it was not improbably connected with the national name Sacæ by which the Eastern Scythians or Tartars were formerly known both in Europe and India. The distinction between the different Buddhas of whom Gautama, prince of Bihar, was one, must always be borne in mind.

derance of the Brahmanical faith. If any conclusion might be drawn from such imperfect premises, it might be supposed, that the inhabitants of Kashmir originally followed an idolatrous system of their own, to which they superadded a few ill-defined Gods and ceremonies, borrowed from the Brahmans of the plains; that whilst they were yet open to conversion, an attempt was made from the other side, or from Tartary, to introduce Buddhism amongst them, which was combated and finally frustrated by southern assistance; the national faith of Kashmir has ever since continued Hindu, and the almost exclusive form of adoration has been that addressed to Siva and his Sakti.

The chronology of the *Rajatarangini* is not without its interest. The dates are regular, and for a long time both probable and consistent, and as they may enable us to determine the dates of persons and events, in other parts of India, as well as in Kashmir, a short review of them may not be wholly unprofitable.

The more recent the period, the more likely it is that its chronology will be correct; and it will therefore be advisable to commence with the most modern, and recede gradually to the most remote dates. The Table prefixed was necessarily constructed on a different principle, and depends upon the date of Gonarda III, which, as I have previously explained, is established according to the Chronology of the text. Gonarda III lived, according to Kalhana Pandit, 2330 years before the year of Saka 1070, or A. D. 1148, and consequently his accession is placed B. C. 1182; the periods of each reign are then regularly deduced till the close of the history, which is thus placed in the year of Christ 1025, or about 120 years before the author's own time. That the reign of the last sovereign did terminate about the period assigned, we may naturally infer, not only from its proximity to what we may conclude was the date at which the work was written, but from the absence of any mention of Mahmud's invasions, and the introduction of a Prithivi Pala, who is very possibly the same with the Pitteruge Pal of Lahore, mentioned in the Muhammadan histories.

Taking therefore the date of Didda Rani, as being at least very near the truth, we may go up the list with some confidence through three dynasties at least. The three last series present an aggregate of thirty-eight princes, and but 409 years, giving us less than eleven years to a reign, an average rate, with which the most cautious chronologist may be contented. The first of the three series, which presents the longest average, gives us less than 16 years to a reign, which is equally unexceptionable, and we have therefore every reason to conclude that the chronology of our author is perfectly accurate, as far back as the year 616 of the Christian era.

The history of Kashmir is too purely domestic during the period comprised within these limits, for us to be able to apply the chronology of the author to the establishment of dates, for incidents or persons of interest in the records of Hindustan. Sankara Varma is said to have subverted the extensive empire acquired by Bhoja, and he may be supposed therefore to have been nearly contemporary with that prince. Sankara Varma reigned from 904 to 922. The date of Bhoja is now fixed with tolerable certainty within the limits of the beginning of the tenth and that of the eleventh century. The *Rajatarangini* however would throw him farther back, if he preceded Sankara Varma and place him in the close of the ninth century. We need not expect however extreme accuracy in this matter, and may rest satisfied with considering it as an approximation to the truth, and generally as an additional testimony of Bhoja's having flourished early in the tenth century.

The reign of Jayapira from 772 to 803 may hereafter throw some light upon the literary history of the Hindus, when the writings of the authors patronized by him shall be met with. It is highly probable that Kshira is the commentator on Amara, in which case, we have advanced one step in the antiquity of that philologist. What author is meant by Bhatta is not ascertained; it cannot be Mammatta Bhatta, the Kashmirian author of the *Kavya Praksa*, as that writer must have been subsequent to Sri Harsha, a king of Kashmir, who reigned about 40 years after our history closes and to whom, or to whose works, frequent reference is made in the *Kavya Prakasa*.

Another set of names of literary interest occurs in the reign of Lalitaditya, from A. D. 714 to 750. Two of the three are yet to be ascertained, but it is highly satisfactory to have fixed the date of so eminent a writer as Bhavabhuti. If Yasovarma, king of Kanouj, should elsewhere appear to be the same as Kirtivarma, it would tend to some important conclusions in this branch of literary enquiry. The state of India at the period of Lalitaditya's reign is tolerably well detailed by our author, but it is unnecessary to examine the subject here, as it has been dwelt upon at some length in the note relating to his supposed military marches.

After passing the limits of the year 616, the character of our author's chronology undergoes an unfavourable change. Thirty-seven princes in three dynasties reign 1797 years, or on an average more than 48 years each, an average term which very much exceeds possibility, and which can only be explained by supposing either, that the number of princes is defective, and that the reigns of those who have disappeared from the record, have been added to those of the princes lucky enough to have escaped oblivion, or that the whole are carried too far back into antiquity, and the date of Gonarda from which it starts, having been made much too remote, it was necessary to elongate the respective reigns to fill up the protracted interval; both these sources of error most probably exist, but there seems reason to suppose, that the first is more particularly the cause of the objectionable duration assigned to several reigns.

The Third Dynasty embraces ten princes, and a period of 592 years, but as one of them Ranaditya engrosses three centuries, the remaining 292 years are to be divided amongst nine kings, giving an average of little more than 32 years to a reign. The most remarkable person alluded to as connected with general history, is Vikramaditya, the second king of that appellation introduced by our author. He is placed in a period new to the many enquires regarding his date, or in the year A. D. 117, shortly after which he must have died, according to Kalhana Pandit. We have no clue therefore to the identification of this prince, and, in the absence of better grounds of conjecture, may attempt it by adverting to the erroneous reign of Ranaditya of three centuries, as well as the long reigns of almost all the princes of the dynasty. It seems likely, that the Vikramaditya, who put the brahman Matrigupta on the throne of Kashmir, was the prince of that name who lived in the 5th century, or in 441[3]; that Kalhana, or preceding writers, confounding him with the Sakari prince, although they did not make him exactly contemporary even with Salivahana, placed him fully three centuries too early; that when they came to the Karkota dynasty, they found out their mistake, and could devise no other method of correcting it, than by adding the deficient years to the reign of Ranaditya, and thus embellishing their history with a marvel. The defeat of Siladitya by Pravarasena as has been noticed, confirms this view of the subject. The Vikramaditya of the 5th century reigned, it is said, 100 years dying in A. D. 541, but according to the *Satrunjaya Mahatmaya* Siladitya was king in 447; we may therefore restrict the father to a sufficiently probable reign of about 35 years, when we shall have Pravarasena, king of Kashmir, in 476. Between his accession,

[3] *Asiatic Researches* vol. ix. p. 175.

and that of Durlabha Vardhana, we shall then have an interval of 139 years, to be divided amongst six princes, and although this will give us a little more than the probable average reign, or 23 years for each prince, yet it still is not extravagant, and the excess may either go to form an unusually long reign for Ranaditya, whence arose the tradition of its lasting for three centuries, or it may be required for the apparent chasm that exists between his reign, and the unconnected succession of the Kashmirian prince, named also Vikramaditya.

By bringing the reign of Pravarasena so low as A. D. 476, we are involved in some perplexity, as to the propriety of subject ing the preceding dynasties to a proportionate reduction. If the series of the princes were accurately stated, this would seem to be a necessary consequence, and if besides this we should restrict the duration of each reign to the highest possible average or 20 years, we shall then effect a very material modification of our author's chronology and reduce his first date from 1182 B. C. to no more than 144 years before that era. There are however some difficulties in the way of this computation :

The first is the reign of Pratapaditya, a kinsman of Vikramaditya, placed however by our author 168 B. C. and consequently, according to him, not connected with the Vikramaditya, from whose time the Samvat era is dated. This inference so obviously arises from the system of our author's chronology, that it is entitled to but little weight, unless that can be proved unexceptionable. We may therefore conclude that Pratapaditya was connected with the family of the Sakari Vikramaditya, and that he lived about the commencement of the Christian era. It does not appear that he was contemporary with his illustrious kinsman. From Pratapaditya to Pravarasena, we have ten princes, and 486 years, which gives us consequently the inadmissable duration of 48 years to a reign. The original chronology is less extravagant, but equally improbable, as that gives us an average of 29 years to a reign ; there is an error therefore somewhere in this part of the history, and either the chronology is wrong, or the series of princes is inaccurate. It is worthy of remark, that the course of succession is a very interrupted one throughout the whole period. Pratapaditya himself ascends the throne without any apparent cause. Vijaya who succeeds Tunjina seems to have had an equally undefined claim. Arya or the resuscitated Sandhimati, was evidently an impostor, who succeeded Jayendra, after an interval, which is not specified. Meghavahana, though called the great grandson of Yudhisthir might have been a more remote descendant, and the period assigned for the foreigner Matri Gupta's election and government, appears to be much too contracted; it is not unlikely therefore that the transactions of the period are imperfectly narrated, and that the blank intervals created by the omission, have been distributed amongst such portions of the record as have been preserved.

The farther back we proceed, the more likely it becomes, that such omissions have extensively and frequently occurred, and accordingly we find the reigns increase very materially in their assigned duration. The average of the 21 reigns of the first dynasty, exceeds 48 years; there are however several chasms in the history, which have been noticed at the time of their occurrence, and it is difficult to admit any very material reduction of the date of the first of the series, in consequence of our author's near agreement with the Chinese and Tibetian writers as to the existence of Sakya about ten centuries anterior to the Christian era. We have only one clue to a reduction of this date: it is possible, that the text has confounded the original Buddha, with the Sakya of the 6th century before Christ. This is the more probable, because from earlier events it appears that, Buddhism preceded in Kashmir the Sakya alluded to. Consequently he could not have been the primitive Buddha, the founder of the faith; if this be the case, we shall reduce the date of Gonarda III to something more than a century and a half subsequent to the Gautama, who flourished about 542 A. C. or to about B. C. 388 and this will leave us an average of no more than 18 years for the reigns of this dynasty.

That Gonarda III reigned about the beginning of the fourth century before Christ, derives some support from the possible connexion between some of the transactions recorded in the history of Kashmir, and those which took place in the neighbouring countries in collateral periods, especially the Turushka or Scythian invasions of Persia.

The temporary occupation of Media by the Scythians, took place according to the most approved computations about the end of the seventh century before the Christian era and they were defeated and expelled about the beginning of the 6th.[4] This period should correspond in Kashmirian history, on the principles we have adopted for its chronology, with the reign of Asoka the third

[4] According to Larcher (*Traduction D'Herodote*) the first 633 B.C. and the second 605 B. C. According to Volney (*Chronologie D'Herodote*) the Scythian invasion occurred B. C. 625 and their explusion in 598.

prince anterior to the Tartar rulers, and we find it particuarly noticed in his reign that Kashmir was overrun with *Mlechchas* or barbarians, possibly some of the fugitives from the power of the Persian monarch, who endeavoured in their retreat to establish themselves in Kashmir.

The Scythian subjugation of Media appears as a single and transitory revolution as recorded by Herodotus, but in the pages of the Persian writers it occurs, only as one of various vicissitudes, in the long struggle for superiority between the sovereigns of Iran and Turan. This war began it appears with Feridun, whom modern writers agree to place about 748 B. C.[5] Kai Kaus according to the Persians, and Cyrus according to the Greeks, invaded the Massagetœ and was defeated if not slain in the engagement. It was in the reign of this prince and that of his successor, Kai Khosru, that the prowess of Rustam was displayed so fatally in opposition to Afrasiab, and the armies of Turan, and whatever Grecian princes may be regarded as the representative of his masters, it is unquestionable that the periods in which they reigned approach to those of the Tartar conquest of Kashmir. Perhaps however it may be still more satisfactorily associated with events, undoubtedly posterior to the wars, in which Rustam's celebrity was first acquired, and may have formed an episode in the furious and for a time triumphant invasion of Persia, by the Tartar king Arjasp. When Khorasan was plundered, Balkh was taken, and the old king of Persia, Lohrasp was included in the general massacre of the priests and followers of Zoroaster.[6] If the king of Persia, Gushtasp, the object of these hostilities, be the same with Darius Hystaspes, as seems probable, these events should have occurred between the years B. C. 521 and 485. By the computation of the Sanskrit text, the Turushka princes must have reigned some time subsequent to Sakya Sinha, who as Gautama dates B. C. 542, but it is not at all clear that the three princes were contemporary, and we have no guide to the duration of their authority, beyond the inferences already alluded to, derived from its ceasing within a century and a half after the death of the legislator. Supposing them then to have been half a century later, they would be contemporary with the war between the Persian and Tartar monarchs, and may have been individual adventurers who took advantage of the temporary confusion to

[5] Malcolm, vol. i. pp. 213, 220. Kennedy, (*Bombay Transactions.*) vol. ii. p. 120.

[6] Malcolm's *Persia,* vol, i. p. 62.

establish themselves in Kashmir. It is also worthy of observation that as they brought with them a new impulse to the Buddhist religion, so the war between Arjasp and Gushtasp was entirely religious, arising out of the attempt of the former to compel the latter to revert to the common faith of their ancestors, very probably the Buddhist or Sakya, that of the Sacœ or Scythians, which Gushtasp had abandoned for the religion of the Medes, the worship of Fire,.[7]

If the Tartar princes then governed Kashmir through the greater part of the fifth century before the Christian era, as appears likely, the accession of Gonarda III must of course be assigned to the commencement of the fourth, and as the year 150 of Sakya or B. C. 392, fell according to the original within the reign of Abhimanyu, we may place it a few years subsequent or B. C. 388.

Without venturing to place much reliance on the coincidence of names adverted to in the note (p. 25), we may observe that both it, and the frequent mention of the *Mlechchhas* which occurs in the succeeding reigns, are favourable to our hypothetical adjustment of the dates, if the barbarians and foreigners alluded to, can be considered to bear any relation to the Macedonian invasion or Baktrian kingdom.

It were too wild an attempt to carry the investigation of our author's chronology beyond the period at which we have now arrived. He pretends not to precision himself. Of the fifty-three princes with whom he has peopled the years that elapse between the first and third Gonarda, thirty-five are without names, and the rest without dates. The singular view he has taken of the era of Krishna will be fully commented on, but it is still too

[7] In the days of Cyrus, as well observed by Volney, the Persians did not worship the elements : this opinion is founded on the account given by Nicolas Damascenus of the pile prepared to burn Crœsus, which Volney infers he derived from Xanthus who wrote a history of the kings of Lydia 40 years before Herodotus ; it was on that occasion, the historian states, that the Persians established the law, conformably to the oracles of Zoroaster, that Fire should no more be contaminated with the carcases of the dead.—*Chronologie D'Herodote*, p. 251. In the code of the Parsis however the other elements receive equal veneration. *Elementa enim omnia tenentur servari pura.* Hyde : *Hist. Relig. vet. Per.* 414. *Persoe nolentes Terram polluere defunctorum corpora non humant*, &c,—*Ibid.* Yet the Tomb of Cyrus was very celebrated, and even Darius Hystaspes himself is said by Ktesias to have had his tomb prepared whilst living—how are these contradictions to be reconciled?

far remote to bear any historical character. We may perhaps however derive from the *Rajatarangini*, a confirmation of the theories, that place the Yadava and Pandava associates within the limits of the 14th century before the Christian era.

The eighteen Princes whose names occur in the list will give us, upon the average of 20 years to a reign, 360 years. There are however but sixteen reigns particularised, and supposing these to be the whole number, the computation is but 320 years, which being added to the date of Gonarda III, as above conjecturally fixed at B. C. 388, gives us 708 B. C. for the date of Krishna and Yudhisthir. But it is admitted that the first Buddha, whose date may be considered at least 1000 B. C.[8] was something posterior to the heroes of the great war,[9] and we require therefore a considerable addition to the years that elapsed between the first and third Gonarda. This addition we may derive from the thirty-five nameless kings, whose insertion probably was designed to fill up the chasm, and will allow two or three centuries to be added to the interval; we shall then perhaps, as a matter of chronological, though not historical accuracy, be near the truth, if we admit the 51 reigns, and give them an average length of 20 years, as we shall then have Krishna alive about 1400 B. C., a computation which will agree well enough with those which have been made by our most eminent scholars.[10]

[8] Buddha, according to Abul fazl B. C. 1366; Couplet 1036; De Guignes, 1027; Giorgi, 959; Bailly, 1031; Jones, 1027; Bentley, 1081 and 1004.

The later date assigned to this legislator undoubtedly refers to a different person.

[9] Sir William Jones says 200 years, according to the Kashmirians, who boast of his (Buddha's) descent in their kingdom, (*Asiatic Researches* vol. i. p. 425). If he alluded to the *Rajatarangini*, and there is no other Kashmirian authority yet in the possession of Europeans, he must have been misinformed, as far as regards the latter part of this statement; the birth of Buddha, either the first or second, being nowhere mentioned in the work of Kalhana, to have occurred within the limits of Kashmir.

[10] Colebrooke supposes the Vedas were not arranged in their present form earlier than the 14th Century before the Christian era; (*Asiatic Researches*, vol. vii. p. 24); but Vyasa the compiler was contemporary with the heroes of the *Mahabharata*, consequently they flourished about the period assigned in the text.

Wilford computes the close of the great war, as having taken place B. C. 1370 (*Asiatic Researches*, vol. ix). Hamilton considers Sri Krishna to have lived somewhat later, or in the 12th century before our era, (*Genealogies of the Hindus*, Introduction, p. 24).

The period that intervenes between the first Gonarda and the colonization of the country under Kasyapa is stated in the original to be 1266 years; that the precise extent of this interval has not been recorded with that precision which the author affects, may easily be granted, but there is some reason to suspect that it is very near the truth, and in that case it is of no small importance, as it gives probability to the whole scheme of our conjectural chronology for the Hindu history, and furnishes an additional testimoney to the veracity of the Mosaic record.

If Gonarda the first lived about 1400 years before Christ, and 1266 years intervened between his reign and the desiccation of Kashmir, we place that event 2666 years before the Christian era, and in fact within a near approximation to the period at which the Deluge may be supposed to have occurred,[11] and to which event therefore the tradition really relates.

[11] The ordinary computations place this event A. C. 2349, but late writers of equal research and various sentiments agree in considering this too recent—Dom Clement. *L'Art de verifier les dates* make its date A. C. 3310 (*Journal Des Savans.* Fevrier, 1820). A writer in the *Classical Journal* (Sir William Drummond apparently) estimates the date 3128 years before the birth of Christ (*C. J.* 24, 153) and G. C. Faber, following the chronology of the Samaritan Pentateuch, places the Deluge A. C. 2938. (*Origin of Pagan Idolatry*, vol. iii. 669). Even then if we admit the original chronology without alteration, it will not be very far beyond the first of these periods, and it comes within the limits of the two hundred theories of Christian writers, which have taken a range of from 6984 to 3616, for the number of years that elapsed between the creation and the commencement of our era.

CHRONOLOGICAL TABLE

FIRST PERIOD

In which the duration of the several reigns is not specified

	Date according to the original	Adjusted date.
Kashmir colonised by Kasyapa	B. C. 3714	B. C. 2666
Fifty-three Princes; names unknown; reigned	Yrs. 1266	1266
Gonarda I Kali. 653 or Damodara I	B. C. 2448	1400
Gonarda II		
Thirty-five Princes; names forgotten		
Lava		
Kusesaya		
Khagendra		
Surendra		
Godhara		
Suvarna		
Janaka		
Sachinara		
Asoka		
Jaloka		
Damodara II		
Hushka, Jushka, Kanishka } Tartar Princes		
Abhimanyu		
Fifty-one reigns ending	B. C. 118	388

The grounds on which the adjustments are made are explained elsewhere. (See *supra.*).

SECOND PERIOD

In which the duration of the several reigns is specified

FIRST OR GONARDIYA DYNASTY

	Years of reign	Date of the original	Adjusted date.
Gonarda III	35	B.C. 1182	B.C. 388
Vibhishana	53	1147	370
Indrajit	35—6	1096	352
Ravana	30	1060—6	334
Vibhishna II	35—6	1030—6	316
Nara	39—9	993	298
Siddha	60	953—3	280
Utpalaksha	30—6	893—3	262
Hiranyaksha	37—7	862—9	244
Hiranyakula	60	825—2	226
Vamakula	60	765—2	218
Mihirakula	70	705—2	200
Vaka	63	635—2	182
Kshitinanda	30	572—2	164
Vasunanda	52—2	542—2	146
Nara II	60	490	128
Aksha	60	430	100
Gopaditya	60	370	82
Gokarna	57	310	64
Narendraditya	36—3	253	46
Yudhishthir	48	216—9	28

Twenty-one Princes reigned ... 1013—3 or 378 years
Average ... 48 or 18 years.

SECOND OR ADITYA DYNASTY

Pratapaditya	32	B.C. 168—9	B.C. 10
Jalaukas	32	136—9	A. D. 22
Tunjina	36	104—9	54
Vijaya	8	66—9	90
Jayendra	37	60—9	98
Arya	47	23—9	135

Six Princes reigned ... 192 years
Average ... 32 years.

THIRD OR GONARDIYA DYNASTY AGAIN

Meghavahana	34	AD. 23—3	—
Sreshtasena	30	57—9	—
Hiranya	30—2	87—3	—
Matrigupta	4—9	117—5	471
Pravarasena	63	122—2	476
Yudhisthir II	39—3	185—2	499
Nandravat	13	224—5	522
Ranaditya	300	237—5	545
Vikramaditya	42	537—5	568
Baladitya	36	579—5	592

Ten princes reigned 592 years and 2 months, according to the original computation; 433 according to the adjusted one, furnishing in either case an inadmissible average.

FOURTH OR KARKOTA DYNASTY

	Reign	Date A. D.
Durlabhavarddhana	36	615— 5
Pratapaditya	50	651— 5
Chandrapira	8—8	701— 5
Tarapira	4	710— 1
Lalitaditya	36—7	714— 1
Kuvalayaditya	1	750— 8
Vajraditya	7	751— 8
Prithivyapira	4—2	758— 8
Sangramapira	7	762—10
Jajja	3	769—10
Jayapira	31	772—10
Lalitapira	12	803—10
Samgramapira II	7	815—10
Vrihaspati	12	822—10
Ajitapira	36	834—10
Anangapira	3	870—10
Utpalapira	2	873—10

Seventeen Princes reigned 260 years and five months, averaging little more than fifteen years to a reign; from the commencement of this dynasty therefore the chronology of the original requires no modification.

FIFTH, THE UTPALA OR VARMA DYNASTY

	Reign	Date A.D.	Date in Kashmir Yrs.
Aditya Varma	28—3	875—10	
Sankara Varma	18—8	904— 1	59
Gopala Varma	2	922— 9	77
Sankata	10 days		
Sugandha Rani	2	924— 9	79
Part'ha	15	926— 9	81
Nirjita Varma, also called *Pangu* or the Cripple		941—9	96

	Reign	Date A.D.	Kashmir Yrs.
Chakra Varma	10	942— 9	97
Sura Varma	1	952— 9	7
Partha, a second time	0—6	953— 9	8
Chakra Verma, a second time	0—6	954—3	8— 6
Sankara Vardhana	1—6	955— 9	9— 0
Chakra Varma, a third time	1—4	956— 3	10— 6
Unmatti Varma	2—2	957— 7	11—10
Sura Varma II	0—6	959— 9	14

Twelve Princes reigned 84 years and five months, averaging little more than eight years to a reign. Besides the Salivahana era, the original introduces with this dynasty a new method of computing, by a cycle of 100 years.

LAST OR MIXED DYNASTIES

	Reign	Date A.D.	Kashmir Yrs.
Yasaskara Deva	9	960— 3	14— 6
Sangrama Deva	0—6	969— 3	23— 6
Parvagupta	1—6	969— 9	24
Kshemagupta	8—6	971— 3	25— 6
Abhimanyu	14—0	979— 9	34
Nandigupta	1—1	993— 9	48
Tribhuvana	2—0	994—10	49— 1
Bhimagupta	4—3	996—10	51— 1
Didda Rani	23—6	1000— 1	55— 4
Sangrama Deva	—	1024— 7	78—10

Nine princes reigned to the accession of Sangrama Deva 64 years and four months, averaging rather more than seven years to a reign.

APPENDIX I

LEGEND OF THE DRYING OF THE VALLEY OF KASHMIR, FROM THE *WAKIAT-I-KASHMIR*

گویا که عالم آب بود وجای برآمدن نداشت ودرمیان اب جلدیو نام دیوی ادم خور سکونت ورزیده علم تسلط وتغلب برافراشت اطراف وجوانب انرا سیرکرده هرجا چیزی می‌یافت خورده وخورده و ویران کرده می‌امد مدتی برین منوال کذشت اتفاقا کشف نام عابدی پسر ماریچ که بعقیده اکثر هنود نبیره برهماست وقتی از زیارت معابد میرفت بکوهی سمیر نام رسیده ان ولایت را خراب یافت و در تحقیق وتفتیش سبب ان شتافت مردم اطراف کفتند که جلدیو نام دیوی است میان ستی‌سر ازانجا برامده مردم را می‌کشد وباز باب میرود دل کشف برحال مردم بدرد امد وهزار سال درموضع نوبدان که مکان مشهور نزدیک هیره‌پور است عبادت کرد ومهادیو که باصطلاح هنود پروردکار را کویند ازکثرت عبادت دریافت او برحم امد ومدعای او را پرسید او استدعای دفع شر جلدیو کرد مهادیو بشن وبرهما را که ازکارکنان مهادیو اند بدفعش فرستاد بشن تاصد سال با جلدیو جنک کرد بنابر شدت اب وکثرت سیلاب دست برو نیافت اخرالامر حیله انکیخت درنواحی باره‌موله لختی از کوه کنده بدررو اب بهم رسانید و زمین مسطح کشت ان دیو را بدست اورده کشت و مکان وسیع از اب ظاهر کردید و بکشف سر مسمی کشت کشف سر کوه را کویند یعنی کوه کشف

The country was entirely covered with water, in the midst of which a demon, Jaladeo, resided, who preyed upon mankind, and seized on every thing and person he could meet with in the neighbouring regions. It happened at length that Kashef, the son of Marichi, and according to some accounts the grandson of Brahma, visited this country, and having spent some time in pious abstraction on mount Sumeru, turned his attention to the desolated appearance of the earth, and enquired its cause. The people told him of the abode of Jaladeo in Sati Sar, and his predatory incursions upon them. The heart of Kashef was moved to compassion, and he took up his residence in Noubadan, near Hirapur, for a thousand years, employing that period in religious austerities ; in consequence of which, Mahadeo appeared to him, and assented to his prayers for the extirpation of Jaladeo. Mahadeo accordingly sent his servants Vishnu and Brahma to expel the demon. Vishnu was engaged in the conflict 100 years, when finding that the mud and water afforded a secure retreat to the Deo, he at last made the chasm at Baramulah, by which the waters were drained off, the demon exposed, taken and slain, and the country recovered and rendered habitable ; being thence called *Kashef-sir*, or the mountain of Kashef.

APPENDIX II

SNAKE WORSHIP IN KASHMIR

We have frequent occasion to notice the important figure which snakes and snake deities make in the worship and traditionary history of Kashmir. The extent and permanence of the superstition we may learn from Abul Fazl who observes, that in seven hundred places there are carved figures of snakes, which they worship. (*Ain-i-Akbari* ii. p. 148.) His statement is in fact taken from the text of Punya Bhatta ; for its being as old as the age of Alexander, we have what may be regarded as sufficient, though indirect testimony ; for Onesicritus, as quoted by Strabo, avers, that Abisaras, who we shall hereafer see is a misnomer for Kashmir, or a part of it, is said by his ambassadors to cherish two enormous dragons, *par ho duo drakontoos apengellon hoi par' hautou pr' esbeis tr' epesthaiton men hogdoekonta pekhon, ton de tettarakonta, pros tois hekaton, hos eireken O'nesikritos.*

Apud quem, Abisarum, *legati ab eo missi, nunciaverunt, duos dracones nutriri, alterum octoginta cubitorum longitudine, alterum centum et quadriginta, ut Onesicritus refert.* The Oxford editor judiciously observes on this passage : "*Serpentes in India nonnulli pedes 30 longitudine æquant ; nulli autem superant. Quo circa hæc legatorum relatio, ad cultum Idolatricum referre videtur, nam Idola esse magnitudinis vere mirabilis, in templis Indorum constat. Exinde Dracones esse ingentes figuras in templis suspicor, et legati vel vivos existire finxerunt, vel Macedones eorum Linguam minus intellexerunt.*—Page 994 and note. R. P. Knight, in his "Inquiry into the Symbolical language of Ancient Art and Mythology," (*Classical Journal*, vol. xxiii. p. 14) states upon the authority of *Maximin of Tyre*, that when Alexander entered India, "Taxilus, a powerful prince of the country" (He was raja of the Takshasilas) "showed him a serpent of enormous size, which he nourished with great care, and revered as the image of the God whom the Greek writers from the similitude of his attributes called Dionysus or Bacchus." Whether the Kashmirian worship of snakes was mystical, at least in the earliest ages, may be questioned. There is likewise reason to suppose that this worship was diffused throughout the whole of India, as besides the numerous fables and traditions relating to the *Nagas* or snake gods, scattered through the Puranas, vestiges of it still remain in the actual observances of the Hindus. It seems not improbable that the destruction of the whole serpent race by Janamejaya, the son of Parikshit, recorded in the Puranas as a historical fact, may in reality imply the subversion of the local and original superstition, and the erection of the system of the Vedas upon its ruins.

APPENDIX III

THE *PANDÆA REGIO* OF THE CLASSICAL WRITERS

In this as in several instances we may trace apparently very different places, some not very far remote, however, and all not improbably resolvable into the same, or at least in some manner connected. We have in the first place a city of the Sogdians, called Panda, as Pliny, vol. vi. p. 16, Ultra Sogdiani, oppidum Panda; and Solinus (c. 49) Ultara hos (Bactros) Panda, oppidum Sogdianorum. The same authorities mention a Gens Panda or Pandea gens, whom Pliny (vol. vi, p. 20) places low down on the Indus, near its mouths. Solinus (c. 52) probably intends to assign them a similar site. Arrian says the Pandæan region was denominated after Pandœa, the daughter of Hercules, it being the country in which she was born, and which he governed *kai ten khoren hinate hegeneto kai hestinos epetrepsen aoten harkhein Heraklees, Pandaieṅ, tes paidos eponumon,* but he does not indicate its locality beyond the remark that Hercules was particularly venerated by the Suraseni, the people on the Jobares, whose chief cities were Methora and Kleisobora, these being in fact the Surasenas on the Jamuna one of whose capital cities were Mathura, and we might consequently suppose he meant by the *Pandæa regio*, the country along the western bank of the Jamuna. The next authority, and who first speaks with precision of the situation of the northern Pandyans, (for we need not here advert to the Pandion of the Peninsula) is Ptolemy; he fixes them at once in the Punjab, about the Hydaspes, the Vitasta, or river of Kashmir; *Peri de ton Bidaspen he Pandoou* (*pandoouon*) *khora, Circa autem Bydaspum, Pandovorum regio*; a place where, aggreeably to the views of the text, we might expect at the period of the history of the *Mahabharata* to find them. That they came originally from Sogdiana would be also in harmony with our view of the subject, and their occupation of the upper part of the Doab is matter of fact. It is also probable that the same race extended themselves south-ward to Cambay and Gujarat, and ultimately to Madura, in the south, known to the classical Geographers, as Madura Pandionis, the various positions being all correct at various epochs, and marking the migratory course of the descendants of Pandu. The accounts gathered by Megasthenes, which are adopted by Arrian and Pliny, of the customs of this country, and its traditionary history, are obviously to be traced to Indian sources, and are connected with the history of the Pandavas. It was the only Indian country governed by queens, they observe. We have a *Stri Rajyam,* or feminine government, frequently noticed in the text but this lay to the east. The notion seems really to have originated in the practice of one woman being married to several husbands, a practice prevailing still throughout the Himalaya and of an antiquity prior to the marriage of the five Pandava brethren to Draupadi ; Yudhisthir observing, in answer to the objection urged by her father Drupada, that they only follow in this polyandrian marriage, the path trod by other princes, *purveshamanupurvenayatam vartmanuyamahe* (*Mahabharata,* Adi Parva). We have seen above that the Pandean country, according to Megasthenes was denominated after a queen who was the daughter of Hercules, a demigod, especially venerated by the Suraseni, and these ideas are of Indian origin although corrupted and disfigured, for Pritha or Kunti, wife of Pandu and mother of the Pandavas, was the daughter of Sura, king of the Surasenas.

Suronama Yadusreshtho Vasudevapitabhavat
tasya kanya Prthanama rupenapratima bhuvi

"Sura the most illustrious of the Yadus, was the father of Vasudeva ; his daughter named Pritha was of unequalled beauty." (*Mahabharata,* Adi Parva). The identity of place and persons is therefore unquestionable ; as to Hercules he may have been readily fabricated out of Sura which, in its usual import means "a Hero", or the Herculean exploits of Balarma may have given to the Greek a reasonable pretext for assigning to him a Grecian appellation.

APPENDIX IV

THE DATE OF YUDHISTHIR, &c.

The original passage is here subjoined together with its most obvious translation, and the chronological results which it appears to authorize.

ashtashashtyadhikamabdasatadvavimsatim nrpah
apopalamste Kasmiran Gonardadyah Kalau yuge
Bharatam Dvaparante bhudvartayeti vimohitah
kechidetam mrsha tesham kalasamkhyam prachakrire
labdhadhipatthasamkhyanam varshan samkhyaya bhubhjam
bhuktatkalat Kaleh sesho nastyevam tadvivarjitat
sateshu shatsu sardheshu adhikeshu cha bhutale
Kalergateshu varshanamabhavan Kuru Pandavah
Laukikebde chaturvimse Sakakalasya sampratam
saptatyatyadhikam yatam sahasram parivatsarah
prayastrtiya Gonardadarabhya saradantada
dve sahasre gate trmsadadhikancha satatrayam
varshanam dvadasasato shashtih shadbhischa samyuta
bhubhujam kalasamkhyayam taddvipanchasato mata
Rkshadrsam satenadvairyatsuchitrasikhandishu
uchchare samhitakarairevam dattotra nirnyah
asan Maghasu Munayah sasati prthvim Yudhishthire nrpatau
shaddvikapanchadviyutah Sakakalastasya rajyasya

Gonarda and other kings governed Kashmir in the *Kaliyuga* 2268 years. Misled by the Bharata (war) being said to take place at the end of the *Dwapara* age, some consider these computations as incorrect. Taking the number of princes, and the aggregate of their reigns, and deducting it from the portion of the *Kali* (that has past) the remainder does not agree with that (that should be left) : abandoning that (computation), the year of *Kali* 653, being passed, the Kurus and Pandus existed. In the current year the 24th (of the Kashmirian cycle) of the present era or Saka 1070, from Gonarda III 2330 years have elapsed ; the sum of the reigns of the fifty-two princes was 1266. Confirmation of the date is derivable from the calculation made by astronomical writers of the motion of the seven Rishis, which goes from star to star (i. e. performs a complete revolution), in 100 years, and the *Munis* being in *Magha*, the earth was governed by Yudhishthir, the era of whose government is 2526.

Gonarda III is the Kenund who succeeds Abhimun, the first prince whose term of ruling is particularized in the *Ain-i-Akbari*, and in the original; the preceding series of princes in both is without specific dates, but as the number of reigns in that series may be considered as either 50 or 52, it so far agrees with that of the first fifty-two monarchs whose names are not recorded, and the aggregate of their reigns although not mentioned may probably be considered the same, or 1266 years. I am not quite sure indeed that the 1266 years do not belong to the series of which the names are specified, and that Abul fazl or his guide have not erred in placing them opposite to the fifty-two unknown sovereigns; however, be that as it may, if we allow 1266 years from Gonarda I, to Gonarda III, and 2330 years from Gonarḍa III, to the years of Salivahana 1070=A. D. 1148, we shall come pretty near to the era of the Kurus and Pandavas as given in the above extract.

Salivahana 1070+78=A. D.	1148	
A. D.	1820	
years	672 ago	
Present year of the Kali	4920 − 672 = 4248 years	
From Gonarda III ...	2330	
Gonarda I	1266	3596
Unaccounted for years of the *Kali*,		652

being the period that preceded Gonarda Ist, but he was contemporary with Yudhishthir and consequently that prince was alive in the year of *Kali* 652, which sufficiently corresponds with the notion mentioned by our author, of the Kurus and the Pandus, existing after the year of the Kali Yuga 653.

A different mode of calculation will come much to the same thing, making however the period close in the Saka year 1073 instead of 1070 as above; what the author means by the Laukika or current year 24, is explained in the close of the history, and refers to the year of a particular cycle peculiar to Kashmir.

	Years
From Gonarda III	2330
From the Ist to the 3rd (Gonarda)	1266
	3596
Years of the Kali to Gonarda I ...	653
	4249
Deduct from the present Kali Year	4920
	671 years ago

Deduct the same from the present Saka Year	1744 - 671 ... 1073
Year of Saka referred to ...	1073 = A. D. 1151

A third calculation turns upon the time specified on the authority in fact of Varahamihara, as the duration of Yudhishthir's era, which according to the opinion of most Pandits ceased with the institution of Vikrama's.

This period comprehends	...	...	2526 years
Added of Saka years	...	...	1070
			3596

The Saka year 1070 (1744 - 1070) was 674 years ago and 4920 - 674=4246 of the *Kali*. But by this only 3596 years are accounted for, and there is remaining of the *Kali* 650. However our author here brings Yudhishthira's era to the Salivahana era, as otherwise the difference between that and Vikrama's or 134 years, must be added to the 650; he also computes the difference between Vikrama and Salivahana to be 135 years; we are then quite in possession of his meaning for :

Years of the Kali to the era of Yudhishthir,	...	653
Year from Yudhishthir to Salivahana	...	2526
Years from Salivahana to our author's own date		1070
Total of the *Kali*		4249

being nearly the same as the result of our first calculation, and but three years more than in our last calculation being the difference required in confirmation of our author's theory. Wilford makes the years of Yudhishthir extend to the Salivahana era (*Asiatic Researches*, vol. ix. p. 211). Colebrooke has given the passage relating to the revolution of the seven *Rishis*, and has described the theory which states it; as has Wilford in the first pages of the same volume (87, 88 &c). With respect to the period of the commencement of the *Kali* age our author's notions are the same as those commonly received.

APPENDIX V

THE WAR BETWEEN JARASANDHA AND KRISHNA

Although the name of Gonarda does not a appear in the *Mahabharata*, yet there is an account of an inveterate and sanguinary war between Jarasandha and Krishna, in the course of which a battle on the Jamuna took place, when Hamsa and Dimbika two princes in alliance with the former was killed. Hamsa was defeated by Balarama, driven into the Jamuna and drowned. The cause and course of this war are narrated in the *Mahabharata* with a great appearance of probability, and throw considerable light on the history of Krishna and of India, in his time; its substance may therefore be not unacceptable. Jarasandha, king of Magadha, is described as a powerful prince; he held in alliance or subjection Sisupala, king of Chedi; Vakra or Vakradanta, king of Karusha: the powerful prince of the Yavanas; Bhagadatta, king of the south and west; the kings of Banga and Pundra, of the Surasenas, Bhadrakaras, Bodhas, Salwas, Paravaras, Susthalas, Mukutas, Pulindas, Salwayanas, Kuntyas, Southern Panchalas and Eastern Kosalas, and he had driven eighteen families of the Northern Bhojas to the westward, and the Matsyas to the south. Kangsa, king of Mathura was married to the daughter of Jarasandha, and it was to revenge the murder of his son-in-law, that the latter levied war upon Krishna. According to the *Mahabharata* this war continued for three years, and in the *Bhagavata* it is said, that Jarasandha besieged Mathura eighteen times. Buth authorities agree in the result. Krishna was obliged to fly and take refuge with his family and followers in a strong place on the west coast of India, where he built the city of Dwaraka. Jarasandha's power was an insuperable obstacle to Yudhisthir's performance of the *Rajasuya* sacrifice or in other words to his pretensions to be considered supreme monarch of India. This impediment was sagaciously interwoven by Krishna with his own quarrel, and induced the Pandava prince to arm in his behalf. Accompanied by Bhima and Arjuna, Krishna entered Bihar by a circuitous route, passing under the hills through Gorakhpore and Tirhut, and he thence appears to have taken Jarasandha unprepared for defence; the text when reduced to common sense, importing, that the monarch was surprised in his capital, and after a conflict of some days killed in single combat by Bhima. The occurrence does not appear to have produced the expected consequence, as it was undoubtedly one of the causes of the great war between the Pandava and Kaurava princes, one of the effects of which was to prevent Krishna from recovering the territory, he had murdered his uncle to obtain. Karna, the illegitimate son of Kunti, the daughter of Sura king of Mathura, who appears to have held that territory after Jarasandha's death, being probably placed, and undoubtedly maintained in it, by the Kaurava princes, to whom he was a faithful and valuable ally. These occurrences furnish a satisfactory clue to the close confederacy that subsisted between Krishna and the Pandava brethren ; his expulsion from Mathura and foundation of a city on the Malabar coast. Before closing the note, we may advert to the mention of the powerful Yavanadhipa, amongst Jarasandha's allies or tributaries ; he is said to possess boundless authority, and to reign over the west like another Varuna. From this passage, and others not infrequent, in which respectful mention of the Yavana power is made in the *Mahabharata*, we may at least infer that the date of its composition was posterior to the Macedonian invasion of India. By the time of the composition of the *Sri Bhagavata*, the Yavanas had assumed a new shape, the name being applied to the Muhammadans, and the feelings of the author have evidently influenced his narration. The prince, who in the *Mahabharata* is a powerful king, and is not otherwise distinguished than as one of Jarasandha's many allies, becomes in the *Bhagavata*, Yavanasur, a titan or fiend who attacks Krishna of his own accord, and whose assault, combined with the approach of Jarasandha, with which however it is not connected in the way of confederacy or alliance, causes the Demi-god to remove his family to Dwaraka ; he himself leads the Demon into a snare, and destroys him. The whole story of the war and the character of Krishna indeed are changed from history to legend in this work, which is manifestly the most modern of the Puranas. The precise dominion of the Yavanadhipa, said to comprise Maru or Muru and Naraka, is not easily identified, although many traces of the former name present themselves, as in the Marucha of Ptolemy, a city of Sogdiana, and in the two Merus, Meru al Rud and Meru Shajehanabad of Khorasan, of which, the latter is an ancient city, its foundation being ascribed to Tahmuras, or in later times, to Alexander, whilst, as the same with Antiochia or Seleucia, it was at one period the capital of the Bactrian kingdom. If the Maru of the *Mahabharata* be either of these, therefore, the king of the Yavanas is the Bactrian monarch ; indeed the same prince is most probably intended even if we carry the application of the terms to a more southerly latitude to which they very legitimately appertain. *Maru* properly means a desert and ill-watered region ; hence it is applied to the sandy desert along the Indus, extending westward to Kirnan and Mukran ; Maru and Naraka may then imply the Sindhic provinces, and these were reduced under the authority of the Bactrian monarch, if we may trust to Strabo and his guides, who state that that sovereign not only held Pattalene, but the territories of Tessariostus and Sigertis along the sea coast. *hou monon ten Pattalenen kateskhon alla kai tes ates paralias ten te Tessarioson kaloumenen kai ten Sigestidos basileian.*

APPENDIX VI

THE GANDHARAS OR GANDARII AND OTHER NATIONS OF THE PUNJAB AND NORTH-WEST OF INDIA

Sindhu-Gandhar, is the phrase of the original—the *Gandhar* of the Hindu writers has been always regarded by them as the *Kandahar* of the Muhammadans, and the text here not only corroborates the notion but by connecting the Indus with the province, shows, that at least a subdivision of it extended beyond the limits now assigned to Kandahar, and carries it across the southern portion of Afghanistan; the Hindu name was known to the ancients, and Herodotus, enumerates the Gandarii, as a people of one of the twenty satrapies of the Persian Empire under Darius Hystaspis, and subsequently as serving in the army of Xerxes. *Sattagudai de kai Gandarioi kai Dadikai te kai Aparutai es touto tetagmenoi hebdoekonta kaihekaton talanta prosepheron, nomos de outos hebdomos.*

Tha. 91. "The Sattagydæ, Gandarii, Dadicæ and Aparytœ, were classed together and contributed 170 talents, and this was the seventh prefecture." Again *Parthoi de kai khorasmioi kai Sogdoi te kai Gandarioi kai Dadikai hestrateu onto.* The Parthi, Chorasmi, Sogdii, Gandarii, and Dadicœ served in the army. Pol. 66. The two last it appears were united under one command *Gandarion de kai Dadikeon, Artuphios ho Aartbanou* "Artyphius, the son of Artabanus commanded the Gandarii and Dadicœ"—*Ibid.* By the Dadicæ were no doubt intended the Daradas or Daradakas with whom we often meet in the text, as the inhabitants of the rugged tract lying west of Kashmir, or the site of the modern Durds. The term however is applicable to any of the tribes inhabiting that portion of the great Indian chain, as its import is merely, mountaineers, and the Dadicœ as the contiguous neighbours of the Gandarii were therefore probably the mountaineers of Ghizni and Ghaur. In Ptolemy's time the position of the Durds, or as he calls them almost correctly. Daradrœ, was pretty accurately known ; he says "*Hupo de tas tou Hindou peges* DERADRAI, *Kai he orane auton huper Keitai. sub fontibus Indi, Daradrœ, et horum montana superemment.* Who the Sattagydœ and Aparitæ were, is not so satisfactorily traceable ; if we may take etymology as a guide they were Hindu tribes : Sattagydœ, may be resolved into Satgerhi, the district of the seven strongholds, a sort of nomenclature very common in India ; and the Aparitœ may be derived from Apara, ulterior or western, or if Aparbartica, the reading of Isidore of Charax be applied to the same people, as suggested by Rennell, we may refer this to Aparbataka, a low-lander, one not a mountaineer, in opposition to the Daradacas or Dadicœ before mentioned ; a more sattisfactory evidence of Hindu identity may be derived from the lists of countries extracted from original Sanskrit works, and published by Wilford in the 8th volume of the *Asiatic Researches;* amongst the northern countries (p. 340) and in a series including Gandhar, we have the Satakas who may be the same as Sattagydæ and in another groupe of a miscellaneous character, but comprehending Balkh, Arachosia, &c we have the Aparitas, a very close approximation to the Aparytœ of Herodotus. In short from these considerations it appears that there is some reason to doubt the accuracy of the opinion entertained by the able geographer of Herodotus, that the 7th satrapy, consisting of the above tribes, lay to the west of Bactriana and Aria, and that the Gandarii may be traced to a town called Cændar on the frontiers of Khowarezm. (*Geography oj Herodotus*, p. 295 *et seq*). There does not appear any occasion to seek for this Satrapy in so westerly a position and as far as the Gandarii are concerned, their easterly situation rests not only on Hindu but classical authorities.

The Gandaritis of Strabo which furnishes an approximation to the Gandarii of Herodotus is placed nearer even to the Indus than the modern city of Kandahar. He observes, it was watered by the Choaspes which falls into the Cophense. He has also a Gandaris which he places between the Hydraotis (the Ravi) and the Hydaspis, (the Beyah) and consequently towards the eastern part of the Punjab. Ptolemy only notices the first position, bringing it rather more to the west, unless as Salmasius conjectures, his Suastus is the Cophenes of Strabo, and making the Indus the eastern boundary of the Gandari. "*Inter suastum et Indum sunt Gandarœ*" The Hindu system agrees with, and reconciles these different accounts, for according to the *Mahabharata,* the Gandhari are not only met with upon crossing the Sutlej, and proceeding towards the Airavati (Ravi) or where Strabo places Gandaris, but they are scattered along with other tribes throughout the Punjab, as far as to the Indus, when we approach Gandaritis. According also to our text, one body of the Gandhari appear to occupy a division of their own, on the last river, which is named after that very circumstance, Sindhu Gandhar, and these may have extended westward as far as the modern Kandahar. Pliny and

Pomponius Mela evidently intend a different people by their Gandari, or more properly Candari, who were a Sogdian, not an Indian tribe, as Salmasius observes, and as is stated by Ptolemy. These may perhaps be referred to the Cænder of Rennell, but analogies resting on a supposed similarity of sound, are very fallacious, as D'Anville has shown, when he criticises Barros for inferring that Kandahar was one of the cities built by Alexander, of whose name its appellation was a corruption ; the city being called "corruptamente Candar, havendo de dizer Scandar, nome per que os Persas chamam Alexandre" (*Decade,* iv. lvi. c. i.) when at the same time he falls into a like error, and derives Kandahar from Kond ou Kand qui dans le Persan designe une Fortress" (*Antiquite geographique de L'Inde ;*) a meaning which *Qand* the word being written *Qandahar* nowhere possesses. De Barros is not singular, for D'Herbelot has the same conjecture, respecting the origin of Kandahar, and he is followed by Meninski, but the name of Alexander is never written by the orientals with the Arabic K, the initial of Kandahar, and it was no doubt employed to express the harder sound of the *Ga* in the Hindi name *Gandhar ;* the aspirate also is preserved in both these words whilst none is to be found in Alexander's name.

The confusion arising from an inaccurate mode of writing or reading names, prevailed as much amongst ancient as modern writers, and in classical authors much unnecessary perplexity has been occasioned, by their erroneously confounding the Gandaritæ or Gandaridæ of the Punjab, with the Gangaridœ, or the nations along the river Ganges. They seem indeed to have gathered scattered notices of places and nations from different sources, perhaps originally tolerably accurate, but which were distracted and confounded in the hands of the writers themselves. Something of this nature occurs in the *Periplus* of Arrian. Between Barygazœ, unquestionably as has been shown by Vincent, Baroach and Bactria, he places various nations as *to te ton Aratrion kai Rakhouson kai Tontharagon kai tes proklidosen ois he Bonkephalos Alexandreia kai Tou ep' ano ethnos Baktrianon.* The author as Vincent observes is a better merchant than a historian, and it may be added, than a geographer, beyond the maritime districts ; his meaning however is clear enough, and he passes from Gujarat to the Punjab, as appears by the situation he has given Alexandria Bucephalos, which according to Strabo was built upon the Hydaspes. Proclis is possibly the same with the Proclais if Ptolemy and Peucolais of Strabo, supposed by Rennell to be the modern Pekheli (*Memoir of a Map of Hindostan*, p. 171). The Tantharagi, Salmasius conjectures with probability to be an error for Gandaridæ. The Rakhosi inhabit most probably the Roh Kuj of the Puranas identified by Wilford with Arachosia (*Asiatic Researches*, vol. viii. p. 336) and it only remains to dispose of the Aratri, which we are able to do most satisfactorily, the *Mahabharata* declaring that the countries situated upon the Satadru (Sutlej), Vipasa (Beyah), Airavati (Ravi), Chandrabhaga (Chinab), Vitasta (Jelum) and the Sindhu (Indus), and without the range of the Himalaya, are all called Arrattas,

> *Satadruscha Vipasa cha trtiyairavati tatha*
> *Chandrabhaga Vitastacha Sindhuhshashthi vahirgireh*
> *Aratta nama te desanashtadharmannatatvrajet*

—*Mahabharata*, Karna Parva. One of their cities, Sakala, is palpably the same with one of the Pandava cities of Ptolemy, or Sagala.

We have in the *Mahabharata* another people of the Punjab, intimately connected with these tribes, the *Madrás* and whom we may endeavour to trace in classical writers. They are sometimes confounded with the Gandharas, but are really distinct, having a different sovereign, and being both separately mentioned in various lists of the northern countries. The nearest classical approximation to them is the Mardi of Pliny, the mountaineers bordering on Bactria, who Rennell supposes were the mountaineers of Gaur.—(*Geography of Herodotus*, p. 283) Rennell following D'Anville infers from the repeated occurrence of this name to designate various fierce intractable tribes, that it was the generic name of such nations. D'Anville too derives it from the Persian *mard*, a man, "un terme qui appartient a plusieurs idiomes de l'orient et entre autres le Persan, pour designer au propre ce que *vir* designe en Latin, se prenant aussi pour l'equivalent de *Bellator*, et meme dans une qualification injurieuse comme celle de *Rebelli*." He connects also the character of these people with the old stories of Martichora the man-eaters of Ktesias, to whom Thevenot found a modern parallel in some Indian tribes of the Dekhan,, and who were denominated *Mardi Coura ou mangeurs d'hommes* by their neighbours. It might be inferred that Ktesias intends *Martikhora* which he explains Anthropophagos, to be the Indian denomination of his man-eating monster, but as he received his fables through a Persian medium, he has retained the Persian not the Indian name (*mardkhur*), from *Mard*, a man, and *Khor*, who eats. For this particular notion, a source is easily found in the Rakshasas or fiends of the Hindus, and the legend relating to the sons of Vasishtha, who were all devoured by Kalmashapada, which is told in the *Mahabharata,* and the scene of which lies in the Punjab, might have furnished Ktesias with the fiction in question.

D'Anville observes "n'est on pas fort etonne que dans un pays ou par un principe de religion tres ancien, l'abstinence en nourriture de toute chair d' animal ert recommandee, il y ait des anthropophages" ; and the incongruity of several Indian customs as described by the historians and geographer of antiquity is in many other instances no less surprising. The incompatibility of their accounts with our received notions, has reflected some discredit upon the veracity of the authors, but making due allowance for imperfect information, and a leaning to the marvellous, inseparable form our nature, we have no reason to accuse Megasthenes particularly of untruth ; of this the *Madri* or *Mardi* will furnish us with an illustration ; they are described along with the other people of the Punjab by Sanskrit authorities, in terms which fully justify the classical writers, and which prove that the various restraints of Hindu polity were either unknown to the north western tribes, or were very little regarded by them ; a few passages from the Karna Parva of the *Mahabharata* will afford to the scholars of Europe an opportunity of instituting a more particular comparison. Karna addresses Salya, king of Madra, to the following effect :—"An old and excellent Brahman, reviling the countries Bahika and Madra in the dwelling of Dhritarashtra, related facts long known, and thus described those nations. External to the Himavan, and beyond the Ganges, beyond the Saraswati and Jamuna rivers and Kurukshetra, between five rivers, and the Sindhu as the sixth, are situated the Bahikas ; devoid of ritual or observance and therefore to be shunned. Their fig tree is named Gobardhana (i. e. the place of cow-killing), their market place is Subhadram, (the place of vending liquor ; at least so say the commentators), and these give title to the door-way of the royal palace. A business of great importance compelled me to dwell amongst the Bahikas and their customs are therefore well known to me. The chief city is called Sakala and the river Apaga ; the people are also named Jarttikas and their customs are shameful ; they drink spirits made from sugar and grain, and eat meat seasoned with garlic, and live on flesh and wine ; their women intoxicated appear in public places, with no other garb than garlands and perfumes, dancing and singing, and vociferating indecencies in tones more harsh than those of the camel or the ass ; they indulge in promiscuous intercourse

and are under no restraint. They clothe themselves in skins and blankets, and sound the cymbal, drum and conch, and cry aloud with hoarse voices; "We will hasten to delight, in thick forests and in pleasant places; we will feast and sport; and gathering on the high ways spring upon the travellers, and spoil, and scourage them." In Sakala, a female demon (a *Rakshasi*) on the fourteenth day of the dark fortnight sings aloud "I will feast on the flesh of kine, and quaff the inebriating spirit, attended by fair and graceful females." The Sudra-like Bahikas have no institutes nor sacrifices, and neither Deities, Manes, nor Brahmans accept their offerings. They eat out of wooden or earthen plates, nor heed their being smeared with wine or viands, or licked by dogs, and they use equally in its various preparations the milk of ewes, of camels, and of asses. Who that has drank milk in the city Yugandhara can hope to enter *Swarga* (Heaven). Bahi and Hika were the names of two fiends in the Vipasa river; the Bahikas are their descendants, and not of the creation of Brahma; some say the Arattas are the name of the people, and Bahika of the waters. The Vedas are not known there, nor oblation, nor sacrifice, and the Gods will not partake their food. The Prasthalas (perhaps borders), Madrás, Gandharas, Arattas, Khasas, Basas, Atisindhus, (or those beyond the Indus) Sauviras, are all equally infamous. There one who is by birth a Brahman, becomes a Kshatriya, or a Vaisya, or a Sudra, or a barber, and having been a barber, becomes a Brahman again. A virtuous woman was once violated by Aratta ruffians, and she cursed the race, and their women have ever since been unchaste; on this account their heirs are their sister's children not their own. All countries have their laws and Gods; the Yavanas are wise, and pre-eminently brave; the *Mlechchhas* observe their own ritual, but the Madrakas are worthless. Madra is the ordure of the earth; it is the region of ebriety, unchastity, robbery and murder; fie on the Panchanada peaple! fie on the Aratta race."
—*Mahabharata*, Karna Parva.

APPENDIX VII

BUDDHIST RELIGION IN KASMIR

The passage in the text adverted to, page 21-22, requires a little consideration both as to its meaning, and the chronological views to which it has already given rise. The text of the original runs thus :

te Turushkanvayodbhuta' pi punyasraya nrpah
Sushkakshetradideseshu mathachaityadi chakrire
prajye rajyakshane tesham praya Kasmiramandalam
bhojyamaste sa Bauddhanam pravrajyorjitatejasam
tato bhagavatah Sakyasimhasya puranirvrte
asmin sahalokadhatau sardham varshasatam hyagat
Bodhisatvascha dese'sminnanekabhumisvaro'bhut
sa cha Nagarjunah sriman shadarhatvanasamsrayo

There are in this passage some obvious inaccuracies and some compound of a purport absolutely unknown to the most learned Brahmans. Taking it as it stood, it appeared to involve the position that the Turushka princes preceded Sakya Singha by above a century and a half, and concluding the Gautama of the sixth century before the Christian era to be intended, by the name Sakya Singha, which is always enumerated as a synonym, the date of Gonarda the third was adjusted accordingly in the preceding pages and placed 640 B. C. an opportunity having subsequently occurred of consulting a Burma priest, and a man of some learning, on the subject, there appeared good grounds for revising the passage, and altering the results, in consequence of which several pages previously printed off have been cancelled, and it is only in the marginal dates of the first dynasty that any traces of the error have been suffered to remain. These are of comparative unimportance, and will be readily rectified by adverting to the table. We have now then to offer a translation of the passage, premising that the term *Puranirvrite* should be *Parinirvrite*, the sixth case of *Parinirvriti*, or in Pali, *Parinibbuti*, the ordinary term used by the Buddhists to express the final *Nirvritti* or emancipation of their Buddhas or Saints in its fullest sense. *Pari* being added as an intensitive prefix. The use of this and some other peculiar expressions, which are at present quite unintelligible to the ablest scholars among the Brahmans of India, but are familiar to the Rahans of the Burman empire, proves that Kalhana the author of the history of Kashmir, or at least his guides, were well acquainted with the language and probably, with the system of the Buddhists.

"They (Hushka, &c) of Turushka descent, were princes, asylums of virtune, and they founded colleges and planted sacred trees, in Sushka and other places. During the period of their reign the whole of Kashmir was the enjoyment of Buddhists, eminent for austerity. After them, when 150 years had elapsed from the emancipation of the Lord Sakya Singha in this essence of the world, a Bodhisatva in this country named Nagarjuna, was Bhumisvara (Lord of the earth) and he was the asylum of the six Arhatas."

As the prevalence of Buddhism and consequence of Nagarjuna, if not subverted, were at least checked in the ensuing reign of Abhimanyu, and as the passage expressly states that the circumstance occurred after the Turushka princes, the 150 years subsequent to Sakya Singha must fall within the limits of Abhimanyu's reign. It is therefore necessary only to fix the date of Sakya Singha to determine that of the several reigns occurring in this portion of our history.

In Hamilton's *Nepal,* it is asserted on the authority of local tradition, that "Sakya Singha, the well-known apostle of the nations still attached to the Buddhist faith, existed about the beginning of the Christian era, he being considered the fifth Buddhist Legislator, and distinct from Gautama, who lived in the sixth century before it." Whatever may be the accuracy of this opinion, it may be safely asserted, that it is diametrically opposed to the notions prevalent in all other regions, Brahmanical or Buddhist. In the lexicons of Amara and Hemachandra, Sakya Singha occurs as a synonym of Gautama, Saudodhani, and Mayadevisuta or Gautama, the son of Suddhodhana and of Maya Devi. A similar string of Pali synonyms is used by the priests of Burma "Sudhodani-cha Gotama, Sakyasinha, tat'ha Sakyamuni ch' Adichheh bandhu cha." The Buddhists of Ceylon also consider the fifth Buddha whom they name Maitri as yet to come—*Asiatic Researches* vol. vii pp. 32 and 414.

Sakya Singha, as observed, is always identified with Gautama. The concurring traditions of the Buddhist nations establish the existence of that prince of Magadha in the middle of the sixth century before Christ. There is little reason therefore to call that fact in question. It is very unaccountable however why

Gautama should bear such a synonym as Sakya Singha[1] and no satisfactory explanation of the appellation has yet been traced; it is equally inexplicable also how a prince of central India, should have borne so prominent a share, in the introduction of a religious innovation, the earliest vestiges of which are so clearly referable to the North West of India, to Bactria or even to Tartary. That the Buddhist religion did not originate in Kashmir with Sākya Singha is evident from the whole course of the history, and all tradition points to a period long antecedent to his, for the date of the invention and its author. At the same time Kalhana, well informed as he is in these respects, has evidently confounded the two periods, and hence assigned to Sakya Singha a date corresponding to at least 1332 B. C., although apparently designating the person who flourished B. C. 542. We may therefore venture to correct his chronology with reference to this latter date, although until we can be satisfied that the Sakya Singha of the North West was one individual with the Gautama of Magadha, we cannot venture to attach anything like certainly to this emendation. Some circumstances in favour of the date laid down are adverted to in the concluding observations, and we may here add, that there seems to be a strange connexion between the circumstances and dates of the Zerdushts of Persia and the Buddhists of India, which deserves a more particular investigation than we have hitherto had materials to undertake.

The passage relating to the prevalence of Buddhism in Kashmir includes the mention of an individual, whose history is fully as obscure, if not as important as that of Buddha.

Nagarjuna as a Bodhisatva (see note in page 20) may be either a religious or a secular character; he was probably the former, as a hierarch, the prototype of the modern Lama of Tibet; his other title however, Bhumisvara may mean a Prince, and

[1] According to the Buddhists of Burma Sakya is the family name of Gautama's ancestry. In the *Parajika Attha Katha* is a very curious account of the four *Sangayanas* or Missions, by which the Buddhist religion was propagated to distant regions. The fourth was of a miscellaneous nature, and included both Ceylon and Kashmir, about 236 years it is said after the disappearance of Gautama; a Gatha or text is cited on this subject which alludes to some legends, that appear not improbably connected with the statements of our history. *Gantwa Kasmira Gandharam, isi Majjantiko tada; Duttha nagan pasaditwa mocheti bandhhana bauhuti.*" Majjantika then having proceeded to Kashmir and Gandhar, and subdued the evil Serpent genius, liberated numbers from bondage.

has probably induced Colebrooke to translate the text generally thus :

"Damodara was succeeded by three kings, of the race of Turushka and they were followed by a Bodisattva, who wrested the empire from them by the aid of Sakya Singha, and introduced the religion of Buddha into Kashmir. He reigned a hundred years, and was followed by Abhimanyu—*Asiatic Researches*, vol. ix. p. 295.

In differing from Colebrooke, there is great probability of committing error, but in this case, the state of the manuscripts, full of obscurities and mistakes, is a sufficient vindication of a difference of interpretation, and until we can ascertain what the reading of the original should be, we may allege in support of the translation above preferred, the following considerations :

1. The ascendancy of Buddhism according to the original, continues some time after Abhimanyu's accession, as well as the superintendance of Nagarjuna ; he could not therefore have been at that time king of Kashmir.

tasminavasare Bauddha'pi pravalitam yayuh
Nagarjunena sudhiya Bodhisatvena palitah

Their superiority is assigned also to argument, not to authority ;

te vadinah parajitya vadena nikhilan budhan
kriyan Nilapuranoktanachchidannagamadvishah

"In that time (Abhimanyu's reign) the Buddhists cherished by the learned Bodhisatva, Nagarjuna, maintained the ascendancy; they, the enemies of the Agama (Vedas) and disputations, overcame all the wise men in argument, and demolished the practices, prescribed in the *Nila Purana*."

2. That the *Rajatarangini* does not mean to include Nagarjuna amongst the kings of Kashmir, may be also inferred from his omission in Abul Fazl's lists, prepared, as those were no doubt from correct copies, and by able Pandits, and corresponding exactly with the Sanskrit text in every other instance.

3. The length of Nagarjuna's supposed reign, 150 years, or in fact its specification at all in this part of the history, is also hostile to its occurrence, as precision in this respect, is affected by the author only from the reign of Gonarda the third.

4. We have the authority of the *Vrihat Katha*, the author of which was a Kashmirian, and lived about the same time with

Kalhana, for denying the title of king to Nagarjuna. His work is a compilation of fables, it is true, and his account of Nagarjuna is evidently consistent with that character; but it still may serve to show in what light that personage was usually considered by the Hindus. In the 7th section of the book entitled *Ratna Prabha Lambaka*, Nagarjuna, is called the minister of Chirayu, king of Chirayapur, a Bodhisatva, a man of singular virtue and charity, and possessing great medical and chemical knowledge. He allows his head to be cut off to save the king's life, whose days his knowledge of the elixir of immortality had preserved beyond the natural limits, and the enmity of whose son and successor, he had consequently provoked; his death however being really brought about, observes the author, by the deities, who could not bear his beginning to render men immortal :

> *evam Nagarjunarabdham martyanam mrtyunasanam*
> *nasodham daivatairyavatsapi mrtyuvasamgatah*

5. Whoever Nagarjuna might have been, he was undoubtedly once a person of great celebrity, for a large portion of the Kali Yuga, or present age, 400,000 years yet to come, is denominated after him, the Nagarjuniya Saka or era; it is singular therefore that there seem to be few or no legends respecting him, and all are but little satisfactory. A Tantra named *Kaksha Puta* is ascribed to him, but his name does not occur in its pages. A work on medicine is named after him, and a Kanara work the *Pujyapada Charitra* makes mention of him, in a similar character as the *Vrihat Katha*, and alludes to him as possessing some magical means of perpetuating his existence, and transmuting ordinary substances to gold.

In none of these cases, except perhaps as the Sakadhipa, does he seem to be considered as a king.

APPENDIX VIII

THE ANCIENT NAMES OF KASHMIR IN CLASSICAL WRITERS

It is said in original (see page 22) that in consequence of the excessive cold, the King resided six months in Darvabhisaradi or in Darva, Abhisara and other places; of a more temperate clime it may be presumed. Darva has not been identified, although the Darvas are in the list of outcaste tribes, and were no doubt a people bordering on Kashmir. Abhisara as well as Darva, must be contiguous to Kashmir, and at the time mentioned, must have been a part of the same kingdom. It is sometimes used, (*Asiatic Researches,* vol viii, p. 340) though not very accurately, as appears from the text, as a synonym of Kashmir, and in that sense it might have been employed by the ancients. Strabo, Quintus Curtius, Diodorus Siculus, and Arrian, with some varieties of nomenclature, mention, Biasarus or Abiosarus, Abisares or Abiasares, Embisares and Abissares, as a Prince, whose dominions lay to the north of the Punjab, confounding the name of the king with that of his country; an error much to be regretted, as it deprives us of the possibility of verifying some of the Monarchs in the Sanskrit text. Abissares as he is called, was the neighbour and ally of Porus, but after the defeat of that Prince, he sent ambassadors to Alexander. His dominions lay immediately above the country between the Indus and Hydaspes, or Vitasta, the Behut or Jhelum; it would have been more correctly placed between the Jhelum and the Chinab or Acesines, but the difference is not very considerable. Abhisara as a part of Kashmir of a milder temperature, is likely to have been the most southerly portion of it, or possibly a tract below the mountains, and approaching the level of the Punjab; a situation which will correspond very nearly with the site of the Regio Abissari of the classical writers. D'Anville finds an analogy to Abissares in Peshawer (*Antiq. Geogr.* p. 14).

Rennell considers Ambisares as king of the Indian mountaineers, the predecessors of the Ghickers, who occupied the hilly tract immediately west of Kashmir (*Memoir,* pp. 109 and 122) and Tieffenthaler calls the Bisari *les habitans des Montagnes de Jambou;* either of the two first positions is sufficiently near, to what seems to be the truth. Although Abhisara appears in the text, in this place, as a part of Kashmir, yet in a subsequent portion of the history, it is mentioned as an independent state, and it might have held that rank at the time of Alexander's invasion; its interposition between the Greek invaders and Kashmir, and finally the southern deflection of Alexander's route, may explain why no notice was taken of that kingdom, in the details of that conqueror's marches, an omission which D'Anville justly regards as unaccountable, particularly as the country appears to have been known by its proper appellation to the Greek writers before the Macedonian invasion of Persia.

Herodotus (*Thal.* 102) describes the northern Indians as dwelling near a city which he names Caspatyrus, and again, (*Melp.* 44) he states that Scylax when sent by Darius Hystaspes to explore the mouth of the Indus, commenced his course from that city. That by Caspatyrus is meant Kashmir seems highly probable from the analogies both of name and locality.

1. With respect to the name it is first to be observed, that there are very adequate grounds for a slight alteration, which will bring the resemblance to absolute identification, with what is asserted to have been, and most probably was, the origin of the term Kashmir; this was derived, it is uniformly asserted by the oriental writers, from the colonization of the country by Kasyapa, the first settlement or city being named after him Kasyapapur converted in ordinary pronunciation, into Cashappur or Caspapur, the latter of which forms, independent of the termination of the case, is the proper reading of the Greek text. Thus Stephanus Byzantinus has *Kaspapuros polis Gandarikt* and Dodwell (*De Peripli Scylacis ætate*) considers this as the same with the Kaspaturos of Herodtus. Wesseling regards it also as a various reading of the same, and although he prefers retaining the latter, he assigns no reasons for the preference. D'Anville also concurs in considering the Kaspapyrus of Stephanus Byzantinus, and the Kaspatyrus of Herodotus, as the same, and it seems most likely therefore that the variety of reading is accidental, and originates with an error in the manuscript; as far therefore as a precise coincidence of name is a proof of identity, we have every reason to conclude, that the Kaspapyrus of the Greeks, is the Kasyapapur, or Kashmir, of the Hindus, which therefore was known by the original of its present denomination, as early as the reign of Darius Hystaspes, or above five centuries before the Christian era.

2. The next question is as to the situation of Caspapyrus, according to the Greek authorities, and its correspondence with

that of Kashmir, and here it must be admitted, there are some difficulties in the way of extreme precision. The general concurrence is satisfactory enough. Herodotus (*Thal.* 102) states it to be in the vicinity of the Northern Indians, and associates it with Paktyaka ; *Alloi de ton Hindou kaspaturote poli kai te Paktuike khore eisi prosorui, pros, arkton te kai Boreo anemou katoikemenoi. ton atton Indon hoi Baktrioisi paraplesien hekhosi diaitan* and in the second, he in like manner connects it with Paktyaka *hoide hormethentes ek Kaspaturo te polios kai tes Paktuikes ges.* They (Scylax and his companions) setting out from the city Caspatyrus, and the country of Paktyaka, sailed, he proceeds to say, towards the east and rising sun into the ocean *pros eo eliou anatolas es thalassan* ; a course, which with reference to its commencement in Kashmir, its progress down the Indus, and its termintion in the Indian Ocean, is so far from being accurately described, as to have thrown a suspicion upon the voyage itself, and which consequently requires some examination.

We may infer from several passages in the text, that the limits of Kashmir was formerly by no means confined to the mountainous belt, which now incloses it, but comprehended other districts, to the south and west, amongst which was Pakhlee or Pakholi, the Pactyica of Herodotus, a tract immediately contiguous to Kashmir on the West, and lying towards the upper part of the navigable course of the Indus, and hence, as Rennell (*Memoir of a Map of India,* p. 146) infers, the country from which Scylax set out to explore the course of the river. It is by no means necessary therefore to question the general accuracy of the account left to us of the commencement of the voyage. Having embarked on the Indus, the course however should have been rather west than east, and this part of the narration is clearly erroneous ; at the same time, as the navigators could only estimate their southern course with anything like accuracy, and as they conceived themselves advancing upon the whole to regions lying farther east, than any yet known to them, the mistake was not unnatural, and need not affect the general credibility of the story. It is to be observed also that we have not the original narrative, and Herodotus may have substituted the popular notion of the eastern course of the river to the sea, for the more correct account of the navigator himself ; such is Larcher's opinion and it seems well founded ; "Herodote qui n' avait pas lu la relation de Scylax, et qui avoit entendu dire, qu' il avoit descendu l'Indus jasqu'a la mer, s' imagina que cette mer etoit a l'est, parce que c' etoit l' opinion de son siecle. Dans un temps posterieur, Hipparque pretendit que l'embouchure De l'Indus etoit a l' est equinoctial." (Larcher. *Histoire de Herodote. Melpomene,* note 95). We may therefore safely conclude that the Caspatyrus known to the Persians and Greeks was at least part of the modern Kashmir.

In the progress of time the name had undergone some change but the situation was perhaps more accurately known. Kashmir appears in Ptolemy as *Kasperia* and is placed with great accuracy Hupo tas t8 Bidasp8 (the Vitasta or Jhelum) kai t8 Sondabal (Chandrabhaga) kai t8 Roadios (Ravi) *pegas* the two first rivers actually rising within the present province, and the third on the confines of Jambu, once in all probablity a part of Kashmir. Ptolemy has also a people called Kaspeiraioi one of whose cities Kaspeira lies lower down and apparently corresponds with Multan (Vincent's *Periplus,* i. 12). The Caspiræi however occupy the country as far as the Vindyan mountains, and the Jamuna. D'Anville appears to have considered these names alone when he declares there is nothing in common with the Caspira of Ptolemy, and Caspatyrus of Herodotus, for as he justly observes the position of a city on the lower part of the course of the Hydaspes, ne peut convenir, a Kashmir; as mentioned above, however this is distinct from the Casperia which lies at the sources of the same river, and the position of which is precisely that of Kashmir. Whence Ptilemy got his Casperia, is not very clear. It is a singular geographical arrangement, that places the same people on the Hydaspes, at Modura or Muttra, and in the Vindyan mountains; the Caspiræi of Ptolemy seem to be the same as the Catheri of Diodorus, and the Cathir of Arrian, who were allied with the Malli and Oxydracæ or people of Multan, and Outch, against Alexander, or in a word the Kshatriyas or Rajaputs of Western India. Hence perhaps the error he has committed in assigning such remote places to the same state, for in the Punjab and Doab, the various cities he specifies, were no doubt governed by Kshatriya, or Rajput princes, although they were not subjected to one common sway, nor constituted the territory of any one peculiar tribe.

APPENDIX IX

THE RAJATARANGINI

From Dr. Buhler's Report of a Tour in search of Sanskrit MSS. made in Kashmir, Rajputana, and Central India.[1]

As regards Kalhana's great Kavya, the *Rajatarangini*, which, after all, will probably remain the only Kashmirian work interesting a larger circle of readers, the Sarada MS. in the Government collection, together with my collection of Ganakak's MS., Sahebram's explanatory treatises and abstracts, the MSS. of the *Nilamatapurana* and other works, will enable us to restore the text and to explain its meaning with greater accuracy than has hitherto been done. The contents of the first six cantos of the *Rajatarangini* were first made known by H. H. Wilson in 1825, in the XVth volume of the *Asiatic Researches*. Next, the text was published in Calcutta, 1835 A.D., by the pandits of the Asiatic Society. Some years later A. Troyer began a critical edition of the text, and in 1840 issued the first six cantos together with a translation of the whole eight cantos, which was completed in 1852. Further, Lassen gave, in his great encyclopædia of Indian antiquities, the *Indische Alterthumer*, a complete analysis of the work; and last, not least, General Cunningham treated its chronology in an admirable article in the *Numismatic Chronicle* of 1848. It may seem scarcely credible that a book which has engaged the attention of so many Sanskritists, and of some of the first rank, is, after all the labour expended, not in a satisfactory condition, and that its explanation leaves a great deal to desire. Still this is the case, and if it is taken into consideration how bad the materials were on which the European and Indian scholars have worked, it is not wonderful that a great deal remains to be done. When Wilson wrote, he possessed three bad and incomplete Devanagari MSS., which were so inaccurate "that a close translation of them, if desirable, would have been impracticable."[2] The Calcutta edition was made, as Troyer[3] states, according to a Devanagari transcript sent by

[1] Published as an extra Number of the *Jour. Bo. Br. R. As. Soc.* No. xxxiv A. 1877.

[2] *As. Res.* vol. XV. p. 5.

[3] *Rajat.* vol. I. p. iv.

Moorcroft from Kashmir, and Wilson's MSS. Troyer's own edition, finally, was prepared from the same materials and two Devanagari copies which Colebrooke had presented to the library of the India House.[4] For the last two books he also used a Devanagari transcript procured by Major Broom.[5] Lassen had nothing to work upon but the printed texts.

Both editions are therefore prepared from Devanagari copies, made either in India or in Kashmir. Not one of the scholars who have written on the book ever saw a MS. in Sarada characters, in which Kalhana's original copy and all MSS. in Kashmir were written. Besides, for cantos vii. and viii., which are wanting in the MSS. acquired by Colebrooke and Wilson, the Calcutta pandits had a single MS., Moorcroft's transcript. After what I have said above on Kashmirian Devanagari MSS. and the difficulty Kashmirian pandits have in reading Devanagari, it is not wonderful that the published text, especially of the last two cantos, should contain many corrupt passages. I must say that I think it wonderful that the changes required are not more numerous. In the first two cantos there are, If obvious misprints and the faulty forms *Gonarda* for *Gonanda*, *Kāsmirāḥ* for *Kaśmīrāḥ* are not taken into account, only between forty and fifty corruptions which seriously affect the sense, *i. e.* one in every eleven or twelve verses. Most of these cases are, however, very serious. The ratio of mistakes does not increase much in the following four *tarangas*. Nearly all the corruptions in these six books have been caused by a faulty transcription of single Sarada letters or groups. But in the viith and viiith *tarangas* the case becomes different. The corrupt passages are much more numerous, and some verses as given in the Calcutta edition, bear only a faint resemblance to the readings of the Sarada MSS. It seems to me that Moorcroft's transcript of these two cantos must have been very bad, or have shown lacunæ, and that the Calcutta pandits have corrected the text in a very unscrupulous manner.

The new materials which I have procured will enable us to restore the text to a much greater degree of purity than could ever be done with the help of Devanagari MSS. But I fear that a small number of doubtful passages will remain, because all Sarada MSS. known to exist at present in Kashmir are derived from a single copy which is 100 to 150 years old. This is the MS. of Pandit Kesavram which is regarded in Kashmir as the *codex*

[4] *Rajat.* pp. v. vii. and viii.
[5] *Ibid.* vol. III. p. iii.

archetypus. It is an ancient Sarada paper MS. written by an ancestor of the present owner. It bears no date, but its appearance shows that it must be more than a hundred years old. The pandits assert that it is the MS. from which Moorcroft's transcript was made, and from which all now existing copies have been derived. I do not feel certain that the first statement is correct, as Moorcroft's copy is said to have been made from a birch-bark volume.[6] The second statement is, I think, true, as all the copies which I have used and seen, half-a-dozen, are new, and agree in all decisive passages with Kesavram's copy. My friends made great efforts to find for me a birch-bark MS, for the loan of which I offered a considerable sum. But they possessed none, and were unable to procure one. P. Chandram told me with a sorrowful face that some years ago he had found remnants of a birch-bark MS. among his father's books, and that he had thrown them into the Jhelum[7] as he had thought that they were of no value. This is the only news of a Bhurja MS. of the *Rajatarangini* which I received, and I fear that there is very little chance of any being found hereafter. The possibility of such an event can, however, not be denied as long as the libraries belonging to the Persian-speaking pandits have not been fully explored.

As regards the efforts of European scholars to translate the *Rajatarangini,* and to use its contents for historical purposes, Wilson's and General Cunningham's results are the most trustworthy. Considering the corruptness of Wilson's MSS., his article in the *Asiatic Researches* is admirable, and deserves the great fame which it has enjoyed. It is, however, by no means free from bad mistakes, some of which, *e.g.* the misstatement[8] that Pratapaditya, the second Karkotaka king, had seven sons, instead of three, each called by two or three names, have been copied by every succeeding writer on Kashmirian history, and have caused mischief in other respects. He has also omitted to make use of the key to the chronology of the Karkotaka and the later dynasties, which Kalhana gives (I. 52) by saying that the Saptarshi or Laukika year 24 corresponded to Saka 1070.

[6] Troyer, *Rajat.* vol. I. p. iii.

[7] It is customary in Kashmir to throw remnants of books into the river, in order to preserve 'the face of Sarasvati' from defilement. The bodies of children that die before teething are likewise consigned to a watery grave. Similar practices prevail on the Ganges and other particularly holy rivers.

[8] *Asiatic Researches.* vol. XV. p. 43.

General Cunningham has supplied this omission in his paper on Kashmir coins and chronology published in the *Numismatic Chronicle* for 1848. The dates which he has fixed for the kings following Durlabhaka require few alterations.[9]

As regards Troyer's work, it is impossible to commend either his translation or the historical and geographical essays attached to it, however much one may admire his patience and industry. He undertook a task very much beyond his strength, for which he was qualified neither by learning nor by natural talent. The *Rajatarangini* is, no doubt, a difficult book, and nobody who attempts to translate it can hope to accomplish his task without making a number of mistakes. But Troyer has seldom been able to make out the meaning of the text, except where Kalhana uses the simplest, plainest language. His renderings of passages in which Kalhana adopts a higher style are invariably wrong, and frequently unintelligible. The worst portions of the translation are cantos vii. and viii. The contents of the historical and geographical essays attached to the translation require no condemnation on my part, as they have been estimated at their proper value by other Sanskritists. But I must touch on one point discussed in the preface to Troyer's 3rd volume, regarding which Lassen also has followed him. Troyer undertakes there, p. x., an inquiry about the authorship of the last two cantos of the *Rajataranigni*, and comes to the conclusion that the author of these cannot be the same person as he who wrote the first six *tarangas*, because (1) he allots to the last two hundred and fifty years double the number of verses which he devotes to the preceding three thousand two hundred years ; (2) because the references and *resumes* made in cantos vii. and viii to and of events narrated in the first six cantos are not exact ; (3) because the viiith canto relates events which occurred ater A. D. 1148, the year given (1. 42) as the date of the book. To these arguments Lassen adds the difference in style observable in the two portions,[10] and that in some MSS. the last two books are wanting.

These arguments, plausible as they may seem, are altogether insufficient to support the assertion made. For, with regard

[9] The necessity of *one* alteration in the date of Lalitaditya and his predecessors, whose reigns Kalhana has antedated by thirty years, has been recognized by General Cunningham himself : compare above, p. 43, note, *Anc. Geog.* p. 91, and *Ind. Ant.* vol. II. pp. 102 *seqq.*

[10] *Ind. Alt.* vol. III. 481.

to the first point, Troyer himself has already given the objection which is fatal to it. If a chronicler narrates the events of his own time and of the period immediately preceding it at greater length than the remoter portions of the history of his country, that is no more than might be expected. His materials were more abundant, and the events in which he himself, his immediate ancestors and his patron, played their parts possessed for him an interest which the more distant times did not possess. This interest which he took in his surroundings explains also why he introduces details which to men of later times appear trivial and uninteresting. To say less would also have been considered an offence against the Raja, in whose employ Kalhana's father was. The answer to the second argument, the discrepancies between statements in the first six cantos and the last two, is that these discrepancies are mostly, if not wholly, due to Troyer's bad materials and faulty translation. It is true that the successor of Chandrapida is called Lalitaditya in the ivth canto, and Muktapida in the *resume* attached to the viiith. But it is not the fault of Kalhana that Troyer has not been able to understand the verses (iv. 42, 43) in which it is clearly stated that Muktapida and Lalitaditya are names of the same person. As regards the third argument, Troyer has overlooked the fact that Kalhana states that he *began* to write his poem in Saptarshi Samvat 24. It contains more than 8000 *slokas*, and it cannot be supposed that the author completed it in the same year. The fact that he mentions in the viiith book events which happened nine years later, in Saptarshi Samvat 33,[11] merely proves that the poem was not completed until after that time.

Lassen's additional arguments are not more conclusive. Neither myself nor the Kasmirians have been able to detect any difference in the style of the two parts. The incorrect Calcutta text is hardly a fair basis for the argument. The MSS., finally, in which the last books are wanting are secondary sources, modern transcripts, which prove nothing.

While it is thus not difficult to meet the objections against Kalhana's authorship of cantos vii. and viii., there are some important facts in favour of it. The first is that the vith canto ends too abruptly to be considered the real conclusion of a *mahakavya*. Secondly, the obscurity of the narrative in the viiith canto, of which Troyer justly complains, is such as might easily be caused in a contemporary history by the chronicler's omitting,

[11] *Rajat.* viii. 3193, Troyer.

as superfluous, details which were so notorious that he might presume them to be known to his readers, or, to speak more accurately, to his hearers. Thirdly, and this is the really conclusive argument, Jonaraja, who wrote, about two hundred years after Kalhana, a continuation of the history of Kashmir, states distinctly that his predecessor's work ended with the reign of Jayasimha, which is described in the viiith canto of the *Rajatarangini*. He says in the beginning of his poem,

> *srigonandamukhair dharmasammukhair a kaleh kila*
> *kasmirakasyapi bhupair apali gunasalibhih* 4.
> *tesham abhagyahemantanisatamasi tishthati*
> *naiva kaschid apasyat tan*[12] *kavyarkanudayach*
> *chiram.* 5
> *rasamayya gira vriddham nityatarunyam apipat*
> *atha srijayasimhantam tatkirtim kalhanadvijah* 6.

(4) "From the beginning of the Kaliyuga, righteous kings, endowed with (*great*) qualities, the first among whom is the illustrious Gonanda, protected Kashmir-land, the daughter of Kasyapa.

(5) "As long as the darkness of night (*caused*) by the winter of their misfortune lasted, nobody perceived them. For late it was ere the sum of poetry rose.

(6) "Then the Brahman Kalhana gave, by the nectar of his song, eternal youth to the ancient fame of these (*princes*), *the last among whom was the illustrious* Jayasimha.[13]

A new attempt to translate and to explain the *Rajatarangini*, and to use its contents for the history of India, ought to be made. But it is a work of very considerable difficulty, and will require much time and patience. As no commentary on the book exists, it is firstly necessary to study all the Kashmirian poets and writers on Alamkara who immediately preceded and followed Kalhana, especially the *Haravijaya*, the *Srikanthacharita*, Bilhana's *Virkramankadevacharita*, Jonaraja's and Srivara's *Rajataranginis*, &c. A close attention to their style, similes, and turns of expression will solve most of the difficulties which arise from Kalhana's style. Next the ancient geography of Kashmir must be minutely studied. Nearly all the localities mentioned can be identified with more or less precision by means of the

[12] *Tan* instead of *tam* is the reading of the Sarada MSS.

[13] In the text the adjective translated by 'last of whom,' &c. refers to *fame*. But the general sense of the passage is the same.

Nilamatapurana, the *Mahatmyas*, the later *Rajataranginis*, Sahebram's *Tirthasamgraha*, the set of native maps procured by me, the large map of the Trigonometrical Survey, and the works and articles of modern travellers and archæologists. But some of the geographical questions will probably require a final re-examination in Kashmir. As regards the use of the contents of the *Rajatarangini* for the history of Kashmir and of India, a great deal remains to be done for the earlier portion, up to the beginning of the Karkota dynasty. Kalhana's chronology of the Gonandiya dynasties is, as Wilson, Lassen and Cunningham have pointed out, valueless. An author who connects the history of his country with the imaginary date of a legendary event, like the coronation of Yudhishthira, and boasts that "his narrative resembles a medicine, and is useful for increasing and diminishing the (*statements of previous writers regarding*) kings, place, and time,"[14] must always be sharply controlled, and deserves no credit whatever in those portions of his work where his narrative shows any suspicious figures or facts. The improbabilities and absurdities in the first three cantos are so numerous that I think the *Rajatarangini* ought to be consulted much less for the period comprised therein than has been done by the illustrious Orientalists named above. I would not fill the intervals between the historically certain dates of Asoka, Kanishka, and Durlabhaka by cutting down the years of the kings placed between them by Kalhana But I would altogether ignore all Kashmirian kings for whose existence we have no evidence from other sources, be it through Indian or foreign writers, or through coins, buildings, and inscriptions. If Kalhana had merely given the stories reported by Suvrata and other predecessors, there might be a hope that we could re-arrange them. But we do not know what materials he had, nor how he treated them, if in any particular case he lengthened or shortened the reigns, and if he displaced or added kings or not. Cunningham's constant search for Kashmirian coins, which, as I learn from his private letters, is attended with good results, will eventually throw a great deal of light on this dark period of Kashmirian history. Full certainty regarding the era of the Guptas, which now seems to be near at hand, will also assist in settling the dates of some kings, especially of Toramana, Matrigupta, and Pravarasena.

For the period which begins with the Karkota dynasty not much remains to be done. The discovery of the initial date

[14] *Rajat*. i. 21.

of the Saptarshi or Laukika era, which I obtained in Kashmir, makes it possible to fix the reigns of the kings after Avantivarman with perfect accuracy. The beginning of the Saptarshi era is placed by the Kashmirians on Chaitra Sudi 1 of the twenty-fifth year of the Kaliyuga, and the twenty-fourth year, in which Kalhana wrote, is consequently the Saptarshi year 4224. For

From Kaliyuga 25 to the beginning of the Saka era is	...	... 3154
From Saka Samvat 1 to Kalhana's time.		... 1070
Total—Saptarshi years		... 4224

My authorities for placing the beginning of the Saptarshi era in Kali 25 are the following. First, P. Dayaram Jotsi gave me the subjoined verse, the origin of which he did not know :—*kaler gataih sayakanetravarshaih saptarshivaryas tridivam prayatah/loke hi samvatsarapattrikayam saptarshimanam pravadanti santah//*"When the years of the Kaliyuga marked by the 'arrows and the eyes' (*i.e.* the five and the two, or, as Indian dates have to be read backward, 25) had elapsed, the most excellent Seven Rishis ascended to heaven. For in the calendar (*used*) in the world[15] the virtuous declare the computation of the Saptarshi (*years to begin from that point*)."

Pandit Dayaram explained the verse as I have done in the above translation, and added that each Saptarshi year began on Chaitra Sudi I, and that its length was regulated by the customary mixing of the *chandra and saura manas*.

The correctness of his statement is confirmed by a passage in P. Sahebram's *Rajataranginisamgraha* where the author says that the Saka year 1786 (A.D. 1864), in which he writes, corresponds to Kali 4965 and to Saptarshi or Laukika Samvat 4940.[16] One of the copyists, too, who copied the *Dhvanyaloka* for me in September 1875, gives in the colophon, as the date of his copy, the Saptarshi year 4951. These facts are sufficient to prove that P. Dayaram's statement regarding the beginning of the Saptarshi era is not an invention of his own, but based on the general tradition of the country. I do not doubt for a moment that the calculation which throws the beginning of the Saptarshi era back to 3076 B.C. is worth no more than that which fixes the beginning of the Kaliyuga in 3101 B.C. But it seems

[15] The word *loke*, 'in the world,' alludes to the appellation *Lokakala*, *Laukika* samvatsara.

[16] *Rajataranginisamgraha*, fol. 4*b*, l. 7 : *tatradya sake* 1786 *kaligate* 4965 *saptarshicharanumatena samvat* 4940.

to me certain that it is much older than Kalhana's time, because his equation 24=1078 agrees with it.[17] It may therefore be safely used for reducing with exactness the Saptarshi years, months, and days mentioned in his work to years of the Christian era. The results which will be thus obtained will always closely agree with those gained by General Cunningham, who did use the right key.

In concluding this long discussion on the *Rajatarangini,* I will add that the specimen of a new translation given below is merely intended to show *some* of the results which may be obtained by means of the new materials brought by me from Kashmir. I do not pretend that all the difficulties requiring consideration have been brought to a final solution.

Specimen of a translation of the Rajatarangini[18]

Canto I. sl. 1-107.

1. Reverence to Hara, who (*grants his worshippers' desires*) like the tree of Paradise, who is beautified by a seam of light emitted by the jewels that are concealed in the heads of the serpents adorning him, and in whom those freed (*from the circle of births*) find eternal rest.[19] 2. May both the halves of the body of the god, whose cognizance is the bull and who is united with his spouse, give you glory, —the left, whose forehead wears a saffron *tilaka,* the colour of whose throat near the ear is fair like the splendour of the ocean-born (*moon*), and is enhanced by numerous tremulous earrings, and whose breast wears a faultless boddice;—the right, whose forehead carries a flame

[17] The use of the Saptarshi era in Kashmir and the adjacent hill states, which continues even in the present day, has first been pointed out by General Cunningham.

[18] The text has been corrected according to two collated copies written by Ganakak Pandit, G[1] and G[2], and the copy in the Government collection, *Ch.*

To avoid confusion in the reference marks for the notes following, the respective slokas are referred to by their numbers.

[19] G[1] and other MSS. read *bhushahina* instead of *bhushabhogi.* Hara or Siva wears a serpent instead of a *jenvi* or *Brahmanical* string, and smaller serpents instead of bracelets. The Kasmirians, being Saivas, consider Siva to be the Universal soul, and expect to be absorbed by him. The preposition *pra* in *pralina,* which adds force to the meaning of the root, indicates that absorption is complete,—*sayujya,* not *salokya.* This verse, it seems to me, is an imitation of Bana's *Sriharshacharita* I. 1.

of fire, the colour of whose throat near the ear is concealed by the ocean-born (*poison*) and enhanced by numerous playfully moving snakes, and whose chest is encircled by the lord of snakes as by a boddice.[20]

3. Worthy of praise is that quality of true poets, whatever it may be, which enables them to sprinkle with the nectar (*of their song*), and thereby to preserve, their own bodies of glory as well as those of others. 4. Who else but poets resembling the Prajapatis (*in creative power*), and able to bring forth lovely productions, can place the past times before the eyes of men?[21] 5. If the poet did not see in his mind's eye the existences which he is to reveal to men, what other indication would there be that he is a divine seer? 6. Though for its length the story does not show much variety, still there will be something in it that will gladden the virtuous. 7. That virtuous (*poet*) alone is worthy of praise who, free from love or hatred, restricts his muse to the exposition of facts. 8. If I narrate again the subject-matter of tales of which others have treated, still the virtuous ought not to turn their faces from me without hearing my reasons.

8-10. How great a cleverness is required in order that men of modern times may complete the account given in the books of those who died after composing each the history of those kings whose contemporary he was ! Hence in this narrative of past events, which is difficult in many respects, *my* endeavour will be to *connect*.[22]

[20] A translation of this verse being impossible, I have given a paraphrase. Almost the whole of its first three *padas* is made up of a succession of puns. Siva is invoked in his form of Ardhanari, in union with Parvati. The words describing the appearances of the two halves are chosen in such a manner that they apply to the female form and its dress as well as to the male. *Kundalin*, lit 'containing a ring,' must be taken as, I think, in the sense of 'earring, or 'necklace' when it refers to Parvati. *Jaladhijachhayachha* if referred to Parvati must be dissolved into *jaladhijachhayavadachchha*; if referred to Siva into *jaladhijachchhayaya chha or achchha=achhadita*. In the description of Siva, *ahina* must be dissolved into *ahinamina*, 'the lord of snakes,' Vasuki, who serves Siva instead of the *jenvi*. 'Near the ear' *may* also be referred to the sentence beginning with *dadhat*. The ocean-born poison is the Halahala which Siva swallowed.

[21] The Prajapatis are fourteen in number. They caused the successive creations of the world.

[22] Verses 9 and 10 form a *yugalaka*, or couplet, *i.e.* they are interlaced in their construction : compare *Kavyadarsa* I. 13, comment. They

11. The oldest extensive works, containing the royal chronicles (of Kashmir) have been lost in consequence of (*the appearance*) of Suvrata's composition, who condensed them in order that (*their substance*) might be easily remembered.[23]

12. Suvrata's poem, though extensive, does not easily reveal its meaning, since it is made difficult by misplaced learning.

13. Owing to a certain want of care, there is not a single part in Kshemendra's 'List of Kings' free from mistakes, though it is the work of a poet.[24]

give the 'reason' alluded to in v. 8. *Yat* must be taken as a conjunction, depending on *kiyad idam dakshyam. Sarvaprakaraskhalite*, 'which is difficult in many respects,' means literally 'in which there are dangers of mistakes of all kinds.'

[23] Suvrata apparently wrote a *hand-book* of the history of Kashmir, to be committed to memory in the schools, which, as usual in India, caused the loss of the more ancient books on the same subject.

[24] Kshemendra has taken care to let us know a good deal about himself and his time. In the colophon to the *Samayamatrika* he informs us that he finished that work during the reign of king Ananta, in the 25th year of the Kashmirian cycle, 1050 A. D. In the *Suvrittatilaka* he again states that he wrote under Ananta, and finally he says that he finished the *Dasavataracharita* in the year 41 of the Saptarshi era, under Ananta's son, Kalasa. Ananta ruled from Saptarshi S. 4, or 1029 A. D., to Saptarshi S. 39, or 1064 A. D. In the latter year he nominally abdicated in favour of, and performed the *abhisheka* of, his son Kalasa. The Saptarshi year 41 corresponds to the year 1066 A. D. Consequently Kshemendra's literary activity falls in the second and third quarters of the eleventh century. The other data which he gives regarding his family and himself are that his grandfather's name was Sindhu, and his father's Prakasendra. The latter was a great patron of Brahmans, and expended three *kotis*, or thirty millions (of what is not stated), in various benefactions, and died a fervent worshipper of Siva. Kshemendra himself seems to have been in his youth a Saiva, but later he was converted to the Vaishnava-Bhagavata creed by Somacharya. He studied the *Alamkarasastra* under the famous Abhinavaguptacharya. He wrote several of his compositions at the request of a Brahman called Ramayasas, and one, the *Vrihatkathamanjari*, at the command of one Devadhara, who seems to have occupied a prominent position in the Brahmanical community of Kashmir. His surname, Vyasadasa, is given in all his works except in the *Kalavilasa*. Conf. *Ind. Ant.* vol. I. pp. 302 *seqq.*, vol. V. p. 29. Kshemendra wrote also, as Kalhana asserts, a *Rajavali*, or history of the Kasmirian kings. The work exists now in Kasmir. But the hope that it would soon come into my hands, which I expressed in my preliminary report, has hitherto not been fulfilled. I do not, however, yet despair of ultimately obtaining it.— Dr. Buhler's *Report*, pp. 46, 48.

14. Eleven works of former scholars which contain the chronicles of the kings, I have inspected, as well as the (*Purana containing the*) opinions of the sage Nila.[25]

15. By looking at the inscriptions recording the consecration of temples and grants, at the laudatory inscriptions, and at the manuscripts, the worry arising from many errors has been overcome.[26]

[25] The *Nilamatapurana* is supposed to have been narrated by Vaisampayana, a pupil of Vyasa, to king Janamejaya. It opens with a question of the king inquiring why no ruler of Kashmir took part in the great war between the Kurus and Pandus. The sage's answer is for the greater part lost, but from the fragments remaining it is clear that it contained the account of the expedition of Gonanda I. to Mathura in aid of Jarasandha, in which he was slain, and of the attempt by his son Damodara to avenge his father's death when Krishna came to a *svayamvara* in the Gandhara country, just as these events are told in the *Rajatarangini*, i. 57-66. A few verses have been saved, which mention the *svayamvara* and the destruction of Damodara by Krishna, as well as the coronation of Damadara's pregnant queen and the birth of Gonanda II. They prove that Kalhana took over some portions of his narrative almost literally from the Purana. Janamejaya's next question is why Krishna considered Kashmir so important as to secure for it a king by the coronation of a woman. Vaisampayana hereupon states that the country is an incarnation of Sati or Uma, and describes its various excellencies, adding that it was formerly a lake called Satisaras. This statement gives an opportunity to introduce the story of the creation of Kashmir by Kasyapa. The Purana then goes on to narrate the 'rites proclaimed by Nila,' which occupy two-third of the works; and it concludes with some miscellaneous *Mahatmyas*. From this it will appear that it is an attempt to connect special Kashmirian legends with those of India proper, and especially with the *Mahabharata*, as well as to supply a sufficient authority for the rites prevalent in Kashmir.

[26] According to my interpretation of this passage, Kalhana used four kinds of records :—(1) the *pratishthasasana* edicts, *i.e.* inscriptions recording the erection and consecration of temples or other buildings and monuments, such as are to be found on almost all temples, religious or even profane buildings (such as palaces), on images, funeral monuments, and so forth; (2) the *vastusasana* edicts, *i.e.* inscriptions recording grants of things, chiefly of land, and perhaps also of allowances, such are found engraved on copper-plates; (3) *prasastipattas*, tablets containing laudatory inscriptions of persons or places, such as now are found sometimes in temples or other public buildings, *e.g.* the Arbudaprasasti in Vimalasaha's temple at Dailwarra; (4) the *sastras*, the works on the various sciences, or, to use a short expression, the MSS. of Sanskrit books, which in Kashmir mostly give at the end some information regarding the author, and the

16 Four among the fifty-two rulers whom they do not mention, on account of the loss of the records, viz. Gonanda and (*his successors*), have been taken from the *Nilamata* (*Purana*).[27]

17-18 Having read the opinion of the Pasupata Brahman Halaraja, who formerly composed a 'List of Kings' in twelve thousand slokas, Padamamihira entered in his work the eight kings, beginning with Lava, who preceded Asoka and his successors.[28]

19. Those five kings also, among whom Asoka is the first, Srichhavillakara declared (*to have been taken*) from the fifty-two (*lost ones*). For his verse is as follows :—

20 "The five princes from Asoka to Abhimanyu who have been enumerated have been obtained by the ancients out of the fifty-two (*lost ones*)."

21 This narrative (*of mine*), which is arranged (*in proper order*) and resembles a medicine, is useful for increasing as well as diminishing the (*statements of previous writers regarding*) kings, place, and time.[29] 22. What intelligent man does not rejoice at such a compilation, which treats of the numberless events of ancient times? 23. When (*the hearer*) has well pondered over the sudden appearance of created beings that lasts for a moment only, then let him consider how this (*work*) is hallowed by the prevalence of the Sentiment of Quietism.[30] 24. Imbibe,

king under which the author wrote, together with the date. This interpretation comes nearest to Lassen's,—vide *Ind. Alt.* 2nd ed. II, 20,—from whom I differ in the interpretation of *sastra* 'only.' He gives too narrow an explanation, considering it to mean 'law-books.'

[27] Gonanda is the reading of all Sarada MSS. Regarding the meaning of *amnaya*, 'tradition, records, see below, i. 45, and the *Pet. Dict.* s. v. The four rulers intended are Gonanda I., Damodara I., Damodara's queen, and Gonanda II. : see above, note to sl. 14.

[28] Mahavratin, which I have translated by *Pasupata*, has been usually taken to mean simply 'ascetic.' I should think that a particular sect of ascetics is intended. A Halaraja, who was a Kashmirian and lived probably in the 9th or 10th century, has written a commentary on the *Vakyapadiya*, of which fragments are still extant; see Kielhorn in the *Ind. Ant.* vol. III. p. 285. This and the following verses show that Kalhana believed that altogether seventeen kings out of the number of the fifty-two forgotten ones had been rescued.

[29] Yukta, 'arranged in proper order,' may possibly mean *parimita*, 'of limited extent.' The verse gives the key to Kalhana's method.

[30] *Santa* is one of the nine *Rasas*, 'flavours or sentiments,' which ought to underlie poetic compositions. Kalhana, who has to tell many

9

therefore, straight with your ears this 'River of Kings,' which is made agreeable by an under-current of powerful sentiment.[31]

25. Formerly, from the beginning of the Kalpa, the land in the womb of Himalaya was filed with water during the periods of six Manus (*and constituted*) the *Lake of Sati.* 26-27. Afterwards, when the period of the present Manu Vaivasvata had arrived, the Prajapati Kasyapa caused Druhina, Upendra, Rudra, and other gods to descend, caused (*the demon*) Jalodbhava, who dwelt in that lake, to be killed, and changed it into a country, known on earth as Kashmir.[32] 28. Nila, the lord of all Nagas, whose regal parasol is formed by the circular pond (*filled with*) the stream of the Vitasta's newly rising water, protects it.[33]

29. There Gauri, though she has assumed the form of the Vitasta, still keeps her wonted inclinations. (*For in her river-shape*) she turns her face towards the ravine (*guha*) just as (*in her god-like form*) she turns it towards (*her son*) Kumara (*guha*); (*in her river-shape*) the mouths of the Nagas (*naga-mukha*) drink her abundunt water (*apitabhuripayah*) just as (*in her god-like form*) (*her*) elephant-faced (*son Ganesa naga-mukha*) drank her abundant milk (*apitabhuripayah*).[34] 30. That

commonplace events, and to go through endless repetitions, is anxious to prove, in order to guard his character as a poet, that his composition is not *nirasa.*

[31] The correct reading in the last *pada* is that given by *Ch.* and G[2] : *spashtam anga rajatarangini.* G[1] has *spashtamarma. Anga* to be construed with *nipiyatam.*

[32] The legend of the Satisaras, of its desiccation, and of the destruction of the demon Jalodbhava (Water-born), who had made it his dwelling and devastated the surrounding countries, is told at considerable length in the *Nliamatapurana,*—see the Report. The gods who assisted Kasyapa were Brahma, Vishnu, and Siva, as stated in the text.

[33] The annotator of G[1] says : *virivishayasthitena nilanagena viranaga iti prasiddhena.* Conventionally the Vitasta is said to take its origin from the circular pond called Vîrnāg or Virnāg, situated about fifteen miles to the south-east of Islamabad, at the foot of the Banihal. Kalhana calls this pond *atapatra,* 'the royal parasol,' of Nilanaga, who is supposed to reside in or under it. The circular from is the *tertium comparationis.* which suggested the far-fetched simile. Regarding the Virnag compare Vigne, *Travels,* vol. I. p. 332.

[34] The annotator of G[1] says; *guhonmukhi—kumarasammukhi kandarabhimukhi cha; nagamukhapitabhuripaya nagamukhena gajavadanena apitam bhuri payo dugdham yasyahsa naganam mukhena apitam bhuri payo yasyah* [*sa cha*]; *yatha gauri parvati, vitastatvam yatapyuchitam ruchim ichchham nojjhati na tyajati svaruchim sedikam* [*svechcham*]

(*country*) is inhabited by Nagas gleaming with the splendour of various jewels, chief among whom are Sankha and Padma, and this resembles the town of Kuvera, the depository of the nine treasures (*chief among which are Sankha and Padma*).[35] 31. To shelter, forsooth, the Nagas, who came afraid of Garuda, it stretched its arms out behind its back in the guise of a wall of mountains.[36] 32. There (*worshippers*) touching the wooden image of the husband of Uma at the Tirtha called Papasudana obtain heavenly bliss and final liberation as their rewards.[37] 33. There the goddess Sandhya produces water on an arid mountain, and shows the presence of merit and the absence of sin.[38] 34. There self-created fire, rising from the bowels of the earth, receives with numerous arms of flame the offerings of the sacrificers.[39] 35. There the goddess Sarasvati herself is seen in the form of a swan swimming on a lake situated on the summit

natyajad gauri nochitam ruchim guhonmukhityadikam vitastatve tyajati tatrapi tatkaranam. The *guha* or ravine towards which the Vitasta turns her face is the pass of Baramula.

[35] The Nagas are the snake-formed deities supposed to reside in the springs and lakes of Kashmir. They appear to be originally personifications of the former. The winding, restless water easily suggested the comparison with a snake. Now the large springs are called *nag*, and the small ones *naginy*, the latter being supposed to be the residence of the females of the Nagas. The Naga Mahapadma is the tutelary deity of the Vollur lake, which is frequently simply called Mahapadma; *vide, e.g.*, *Srikanthacharita* III. 9, and Jonaraja thereon. Sankhanaga resides, according to Sahebram's *Tirthasamgraha*, in a lake near Dharindha in the Lar pargana.

[36] Kashmir is here personified and supposed to face Garuda, who chased the Nagas through the 'Gate' of the Valley at Baramula. Under this supposition it becomes intelligible how the mountain-chains surrounding the country can be likened to 'arms stretched out behind the back.' The story of the Nagas' flight to Kashmir occurs in the *Nilamatapurana*.

[37] The locality intended is the Papasudana Naga or Kapatesvara Tirtha, said to be in the Kotahara pargana near Islamabad,—*Kapatesvara, Kotihiragrame Kotaharakhyavishaye,* G[1]. Comp. *srikanthachar.* iii. 14, where the other name of the Tirtha, Kapatesvara, is given.

[38] *Bhranganamavishye devalagramasamipasthale,* G[1]. The story how a certain Mayavatu, son of Bhadresvaravatu, brought the goddess Samdhya-Ganga to his *asrama* near Deval, in the Bhring pargana, is told at length in the *Samdhyamahatmya.*

[39] The Svayambhu Agni here mentioned is the burning naphtha spring in Kamraj or Kramarajya, near Sopur. So also G[1]—*Kramarajye svaimiti prasiddhah,* and Sahebram, *Tirthasamgraha.*

of Mount Bheda, which is sanctified by the source of Ganga.[40] 36. There, even now, drops of sandal-ointment offered by the gods are to be seen in Nandikshetra, in the temple, the habitation of the immortals.[41] 37. There, after looking on the goddess Sarada (*the worshipper*) at once reaches the river Madhumati and Sarasvati who is worshipped by poets.[42] 38. In that (*country*) which is adorned by Kesava-Chakrabhrit, and by Siva-Vijayesa and other (*deities*), there is not a space as large as a grain of sesamum which has not its Tirtha.[43] 39. The country may be gained by the strength of spiritual merit, but not by armies of soldiers. Hence people there are chiefly anxious about the next world. 40. There the rivers are free from dangers and aquatic monsters, provided with warm bath-houses for the winter, and comfortable places (*for descending*) into the current. 41. Out of respect, as it were, the Sun does not fiercely shine, during summer even, in that (*country*) which has been created by his father, as he knows that it ought not to be tormented. 42. Things that elsewhere in the three worlds are difficult to find, viz. lofty halls of learning, safforn, icy water, and grapes, are common there. 43. In these three worlds the jewel-producing region of Kuvera is (*chiefly*) worthy of praise; (*next*) in that (*region*) the mountain range, the father of Gauri; and (*thirdly*) the country which is enclosed by that (*mountain*).[44]

44. Fifty-two princes, beginning with Gonanda, who in the Kâliyuga were contemporaries of the Kurus and of the sons of

[40] *Bhedagiri—bhedabhrandu iti prasiddah*, G[1].—The *Gangamahatmya*, No. 56, mentions the hill.

[41] *Nandikshetra naranamagrame*, G[1]. It is situated in the Lar pargana, not far from the Haramukutaganga, and is a station on the pilgrimage to the latter; see also *Jour. As. Soc. Beng.* vol. xxxv. p. 226. So also Sahebram's *Tirthasamgraha*. Suravasaprasada *may* be a noun proper.

[42] *Srisaile harel iti prasiddhe sthale daraddesasamipavartini*, G[1]. Horil is found on the Survey map in the pargana Khuyaham, to the north of the Vollur lake, into which latter the Madhumati falls, as marked on the native map. Sahebram (*Tirthasamgraha*) places these *tirthas* in Lolab.

[43] *Chakrabhrit kesavah chakradhara iti prasiddhah; vijayesa isana bijyabrar iti prasiddhah*, G[1]. The ancient fane of Vishnu-Chakradhara lay on a low hill, situated about a mile below Bijbror, on the left bank of the Vitasta, and is now called Chakdhar. See Report, p. 18. Bijbror or Bijbihar is too well known to need any further notice. But compare Vigne, vol. II. p. 23.

[44] The father of Gauri, *i.e.* the Himalaya.

Kunti, have not been recorded.[45] 45. In consequence of the demerit of those rulers of the land of Kasyapa, no poets of creative power, who produced their bodies of glory, existed in those times. 46. We pay reverence to that naturally sublime craft of poets, without whose favour powerful princes are not remembered, although the earth that is girdled by the oceans was sheltered under the protection of their arms as in the shade of a forest. 47. Without thee, O brother composer of true poetry, this world does not even dream of the existance of its chiefs, though they rested their feet on the temples of elephants, though they won prosperity, though maidens, moons of the day, dwelt in their palaces.—without thee the universe is blind : why (*praise*) thee with a hundred hymns?

48-49. Some (*authors*) have given this (*following*) calculation of the years wrongly, as they were deceived by the statement that Gonanda and his successors protected Kashmir during twenty-two hundred and sixty-eight years in the Kaliyuga, (*and*) that the Bharata (*war*) took place at the end of the Dvapara yuga.[46] 50. If the years of the kings, the length of whose reigns is known, are added together (*and deducted*) from the past period of the Kaliyuga diminished by that (*time which elapsed between the beginning* of the Kaliyuga and the Bharata war), no rest remains.[47] 51. When six hundred and fifty-three years of the *Kaliyuga* had passed away, the Kurus and Pandavas lived on the earth. 52. At present, in the twenty-fourth year (*of*) the Laukika (*era*), one thousand and seventy years of the Saka era have passed.[48] 53. On the whole, at that (*time*) two thousand three hundred and thirty years have elapsed since (*the times of*) Gonanda (*III.*). 54. Twelve hundred and sixty-six years are supposed (*to be comprised*) in the sum of the reigns of those fifty-two kings. 55. Since the Great Bear moves in a hundred

[45] Kuvera is the regent of the North, and the possessor of the nine treasures.

[46] In the text read *Kásmiran. Kásmira* : not Kasmeera is the form which the Sarada MSS. give everywhere. The two verses form a *yugalaka* or *yugma*, and v. 48 must therefore be taken as depending on the words *iti varttaya vimohitah*, which occur in the second half of v. 49.

[47] I am unable to make anything of this verse, except by taking *tad* in *tadvivarjitat* to refer to *bharatam* in v. 49. For with any other explanation the figures must come wrong and the verse must be taken as part of the *purvapaksha*, which it is not, as the opinion of the 'some' has been done with in the preceding verses.

[48] Regarding the Laukika or Saptarshi era see above.

years from one Nakshatra to the other, the author of the (*Brihat*) *Samhita* has thus given his decision regarding its motion in this (*verse*)[49]—

56. "When king Yudhishthira ruled the earth, the Munis (*the Great Bear*) stood in (*the Nakshatra*) Maghah. His reign fell 2526 years (*before*) the Saka era."[50]

57. The brave king of Kashmir, Gonanda, was worshipped by the region (*of the North*), which Kailasa illuminates (*with the glitter of its snow*), and rolling Ganga clothes with a soft and transparent garment.[51]

58. The earth, afraid as it were that Sesha's poison might be infused into her, left the serpent's body and rested in the

[49] The proper reading, instead of the *Uchare*, of the Calcutta and Paris editions, is *Tachare*, which is found in all Sarada MSS. The mistake has been caused by the resemblance of Sarada *u* and *ta*.

[50] The verse is found in *Brihat Samhita* xiii. 3. *Jour. R. As. Soc.* N. S. vol. v. p. 79. From vv. 48-56, which give the chronological basis of the *Tarangini*, it would appear that the statement of the *Nilamata*, which makes Gonanda II. contemporary with the Kurus and Pandavas, was the starting-point common to Kalhana and other chronologists. But while others placed Gonanda in the beginning of the Kaliyuga, guided by the tradition that the Great War occurred at the end of the Dvapara-yuga, Kalhana used Varahamihira's date of Yudhishthira, 2526 before Saka, or 653 Kali, to determine the beginning of the Gonandas. He then cut down or lengthened (*vide* above, v. 21) the reigns of the Kasmirian kings until their sum total *plus* 653 agreed with the time which had elapsed between the year in which he began to write, viz. 1070, and the beginning of the Kaliyuga. His equation, as has been shown by Wilson, Troyer, and others is—

Years of the Kaliyuga—elapsed in Saka 1070=1070. From Gonanda III. +3179=4249.

52 lost kings of Kashmir—1266 (v. 54)+2330 (v. 53)+653 (v. 51) =4249.

The expression *prayah*, 'on the whole' (v. 53), and '*matah* (v. 54), seem to me further proof (in addition to the direct statement. v. 21) that Kalhana did make alterations in the length of the reigns. Another circumstance shows with what levity Kalhana worked. The period of 1266 years begins with the reign of Gonanda I., and Gonanda II., his grandson, was, according to the Purana, the infant king when the Great War began. Nevertheless he assumes that the coronation of Yudhishthira occurred in the first year of Gonanda I., as he places the whole of the 1266 years after Kali 653, in which Yudhishthira was installed on the throne, according to Varahamihira.

[51] This as well as the subsequent stories regarding Damodara and Gonanda II. down to v. 82 are taken from the *Nilamatapurana*.

king's arm that was adorned by the jewel sacred to Garuda.[52] 59. Jarasandha, his relation, called on him for help. With a a large army of he besieged Mathura (*the town*) of Krishna. 60. When he pitched his camp on the banks of the Kalindi, the fame of (*the hostile*) warriors vanished together with the smiles of the females of Yadu's race. 61. Once (*Balarama*), whose ensign is the plough, engaged that warrior in battle in order to protect his entirely shattered forces. 62. The bridal wreath of the goddess of victory faded, since it remained long in her hands, while these warriors of equal strength were combating each other and the result was doubtful. 63. Finally, with limbs wounded by each other's weapons, the king of Kashmir embraced the earth, and the scion of Yadu the goddess of victory.

64. When that brave warrior travelled the road which great heroes easily find, his son, the illustrious Damodara, protected the earth.[53] 65. That proud prince, though he had obtained a kingdom which was distinguished by affording the means of enjoyment, found no peace because he brooded over the death of his father.[54] 66. Then that (*hero*) whose arm, (*strong*) like a tree, was burning with pride, heard that the Vrishnis had been invited by the Gandharas on the banks of the Indus to an approaching *svayamvara*, and that they had come.[55] 67. Then, (*impelled*) by excessive fury, he undertook on their approach an expedition against them, obscuring the sky with the dust that the horses of his army raised. 68. In the battle with those (*foes*), the bride, who was about to choose a husband and was impatient for the wedding, was slain. Then the celestial maidens chose husbands in Gandharaland.[56] 69. Then the valiant ruler of the earth-disc, attacking, in the battle with the god whose

[52] The jewel sacred to Garuda, the destroyer of the Serpents, is the emarald. Read *Deham* with the Sar. MSS. instead of the nonsensical *Desam* of the editions.

[53] The road to Svarga is meant.

[54] Read here and elsewhere with the Sarada MSS., *Kasmirik* instead of *Kasmirak* :

[55] Regarding the Gandharas on the Sindhu see Cunningham, *Anc. Geog.* pp. 47 *seqq.* Vrishni is another name of the Yadavas. In the text read *Darponadordam* :

[56] The editions read *Nighanatisma*, a corruption of which is also found in *Ch*, ; G[1] reads *Nighyatesma*. The former reading gives no sense. *Nighnyate* is apparenty intended for *nihanyate*, and it is just possible that Kalhana used this incorrect form on account of the metre.

weapon is the war-disc, the disc-like array of his enemies, went to heaven by the road of the edge of the battle-disc.[57]

70. Then Krishna, the descendant of Yadu, ordered the Brahmans to install the (*king's*) pregnant widow Yasovati on the throne. 71. When the servants of the *slayer of Madhu* at that time became angry, he reciting this stanza from the Purana, reproved them :

72. "Kashmir-land is Parvati ; know that its king is a portion of Siva. Though he be wicked, a wise man who desires (*his own*) welfare will not despise him."

73. The eyes of men, who formerly regarded with contempt (*the country and the queen*) as two females and objects of enjoyment, looked (*after this speech was uttered*) upon (*Yasovati*) as the mother of her subjects, and (*upon the country*) as a goddess.[58]

74. Then in the proper month that queen bore a son endowed with divine marks, a new sprout of the family tree which had been consumed by fire.

75. The Brahmans performed the coronation and kindred rites for him together with his *jatakarma* and other sacraments.

76. The infant king received afterwards, together with the regal dignity, the name of his grandfather, Gonanda.[59] 77. Two nurses were engaged in rearing him, that one gave her milk, the other complete prosperity.[60] 78. The ministers of his father, who were careful that his being pleased should not remain without results, bestowed wealth upon his attendants even when he smiled without cause.[61] 79. When his officers, unable to

[57] The numerous puns on the word *chakra*, 'disc,' make this verse dear to the pandit. *Chakradharadhvana*, 'by the road of the edge of the battle-disc,' may also be dissolved, *chakradharah krishnah, sa eva panthastena* and be translated 'the road (being opened to him by) Krishna, the bearer of the war-disc.' To be slain by a person as holy as Krishna would, of course, ensure heaven to the victim. Perhaps Kalhana intended it to be taken both ways.

[58] The earth, or the country, is always considered to be the *wife* of the king.

[59] Read with the Sarada MSS.. *Nerandrasriya*, instead of *Nagendrasriya* as Troyer and the Calcutta edition have.

[60] The second nurse is the *earth*, or the country, which gave him entire prosperity.

[61] It is the custom and the duty of kings to give presents whenever they are pleased. The ministers watched lest the custom should be neglected in the case of the infant king, and gave presents whenever he smiled.

understand his infant stammering, did not fulfil his orders, they considered themselves guilty of a crime. 80. When the infant king ascended his father's throne, he whose legs were dangling in the air did not banish (*from the hearts of his subjects*) the desire (*to prostrate themselves*) before his footstool.[62] 81. When the ministers decided the legal and religious disputes of the subjects, they listened to (*the opinion of the child*) whose locks were moved by the wind from the *chauris*. 82. Thus (*it happened that*) the king of Kashmir, being an infant, was taken neither by Kurus nor Pandavas to assist them in the Great War.

83. Thirty-five kings who followed him, and whose names and deeds have perished in consequence of the loss of the records, have been immersed in the ocean of oblivion.

84. After them Lava, an ornament of the earth, a favourite of Victory that is clothed in a flowing robe of fame, became king. 85. The roar of his army, which roused the universe from its slumber, sent—O wonder!—his enemies to their long slumber. 86. Constructing eighty-four lakhs of stone buildings, he founded the town of Lolora.[63] 87. After giving to a community of Brahmans the *agrahara* of Levara on the Lidar, the valiant (*king*) endowed with blameless heroism and splendour ascended to heaven.[64]

88. He was succeeded by his son Kusa, expert in (*deeds of*) prowess and lotus-eyed, who gave the *agrahara* of Kuruhara.[65]

89. After him his son, the illustrious Khagendra, the destroyer of his foes' elephants, the first (*among men*), an abode of valour, obtained the throne. 90. He settled the two principal *agraharas* (*of Kashmir*), Khagi and Khonamusha, and afterwards he

[62] Read *Hrita* with the Sarada MSS. instead of *Krita*. *Utkantha padapithasya*, 'the desire for the footstool,' means the desire to use the footstool or its legitimate purposes, *i.e.* for touching it with the forehead. The persons from whom this desire was *not* taken are not named. Hence it must be understood that everybody, all the king's subjects, are meant. The verse is intended to furnish another proof that this infant king was respected quite as much as any grown-up ruler could have been.

[63] Lolora is situated in the pargana of Lolab.

[64] The Ledari, now called Lidar or Lidder, is the principal northern tributary of the Vitasta, which it joins not far from Bijbror. An *agrahara* is an *inam* village given to a Brahman, or to a community of Brahmans. See the *Pet. Dict. s. v.* Levara is said to exist now.

[65] According to the annotator of G^1, Kuruhara is now called Kular, and Pandit Dayaram places it in the Dachhinpara pargana.

ascended to that world which he had bought by deeds brilliant like (*the glitter of*) Siva's (*teeth in*) smiling.[66]

91. After him came his son Surendra, possessed of priceless greatness, who was an entire stranger to guilt, who far surpassed Indra's state, and whose deeds astonished the world.[67] 92. Surendra, the lord of the gods, could not be compared to this Surendra, since he is called *satamanyu*, 'the harbourer of a hundred grudges,' and *gotrabhit*, 'the destroyer of the gotra,' while (Surendra *of* Kashmir) deserved the surname *santamanyu*, 'he whose anger is appeased,' and *gotrarakshi*, 'the protector of the gotra.'[68] 93. That illustrious (*ruler*) founded on the frontiers of Dardistan a town called Sauraka and a *vihara* called Narendrabhavana.[69] 94. In his own kingdom that prince of great fame and of holy works founded a *vihara*, called Saurasa, which became famous for piety.

95. After this king had died without issue, Godhara, a scion of a different family, protected the earth, together with the best of mountains.[70] 96. Liberal, pious Godhara went to heaven after presenting the *agrahara* Hastisala to the Brahmans.[71]

[66] Khagi is said to be the modern Kakapur (Wilson and Troyer), and Khonamusha is Khunmoh, as was first recognized by General Cunningham. See also above Report, pp. 4 *seqq.* The Sarada MSS. read Khonamusha instead of Khunamusha, and to this form points also the Khonamukha of Bilhana, *Vikramankacharita*, xviii. 7. As there is hardly any difference between the pronunciation of *o* and *u* in Kashmir the spelling does not matter much.

[67] *Dirghamaghavattavahishkritah*, of which a double translation has been given, may be taken as two words, *dirgham* and *aghavattavahiskritah*, or as a compound, *dirgha-maghavatta-vahishkritah*. The author, like a good Kavi, loves his pun dearly, and intends it to be taken both ways.

[68] Indra or Surendra is called Gotrabhit because he opened the *gotra* or pen in which the Panis had confined the cows of the gods : see the quotations in the *Pet. Dict.* s. v. In the case of the Kashmirian Surendra, *gotra* must be taken to mean his own or the Brahmanical families.

[69] Neither the places mentioned in this verse nor the one mentioned in the text can be traced, though the former, as they were situated on the frontier of Dardistan, must have been somewhere in Lolab or Khuyaham. It is important to note that Kalhana ascribes the foundation of *viharas*, or Bauddha monasteries, to the last king of the line of Gonanda, whom he must have placed somewhere about the 18th century before our era.

[70] Read with *Ch.* and G[1] *Sabhudharabaram dharam* 'The best of mountains' is the Himalaya.

[71] According to the annotator of G[1], Hastisala is now called

97. His son Suvarna after him distributed gold (*suvarna*) to the needy, he who caused to flow, in the district of Karala, the brook Suvarnamani.[72]

98. His son Janaka, comparable to a father (*janaka*) of his subjects, founded the *vihara* and *agrahara* called Jalora.[73]

99. After him the illustrious Sachinara, whose disposition was forgiving, protected the earth as ruler, his commands gaining obedience (*from all*). 100. That king founded the two *agraharas* Samanjasa and Asanara. Without male issue he obtained half of Indra's seat (*after death*).[74]

101. Next, the son of that king's grand-uncle, and great-grandson of Sakuni, the veracious Asoka, ruled the earth. 102. That king, cleansed from sin and converted to the teaching of Jina, covered Sushkaletra and Vitastatra with numerous *stupas*.[75] 103. Within the precincts of the Dharmaranya Vihara in Vitastatrapura stood a *chaitya*, built by him, the height of which the eye was unable to measure.[76] 104. That illustrious prince built the town of Srinagari, which is most important on account of its nine million and six hundred thousand houses.[77] 105. This virtuous (*prince*) removed the old brick enclosure of the temple of Vijayesvara, and built a new one of stone.[78]

Asthihil. My Brahman friends did not know this latter name, and thought that Hashir might be meant.

[72] The annotator of G[1] explains Karale by *ardhavane*, and *Suvarnamanikulya* by *Sunnamaya nado*, the *nala* or brook called Sunnamaya, marked on the native map in the pargana Adhvan or Arwin.

[73] My Kashmirian friends identify Zavur, near Zevan, with Jalora.

[74] According to the annotator of G[1] the modern equivalent of Samangasa is Svangas, in the Kotahara pargana, near Islamabad, and of Asanara, the well-known village of Chrar.

[75] Read *Sushkaletrabitastatrau*. The annotator of G[1] remarks : *sushkaletrah hukhletra vitastatra vithavatra, sushkaletrascha vitastatrascha tau sushkaletravitastatrau dvitiyadvivachanam etat*. Both localities, the names of which are usually pronounced *Hoklitr* and *Vethvotr*, are situated in the Devasar pargana to the south of Islamabad. The former is marked on the Trig. Surv. map as Vithawiter.

[76] Read *Jatkritam* with G[1] and *Ch*. instead of the *Jatkrityam* of the editions.

[77] General Cunningham (*Anc. Geog.* p. 95) has fixed the site of the ancient Srinagari near Pandrethan (Puranadhishthana). Some Pandits think that it lay near Islamabad.

[78] Regarding the very remarkable *prakaras* of the Kashmirian temples see Cunningham, *Jour. As Soc. Beng.* vol. xiii. pp. 340 *seqq.*

106. He whose dejection had been overcome built within the enclosure of Vijayesvara, and near it, two (*other*) temples, which were styled Asokesvara.[79] 107. As the country was overrun by Mlechhas, the pious (*king*) obtained from Siva, the lord of creatures, a son in order to destroy them.[80]

[79] *Asokesvara* must be explained as a *madhyamapadalopi* compound by *Asokena nirmita isvara*, 'the (temple of) Siva built by Asoka.' The same remark applies to the numerous names of temples ending in Isvara and beginning with the name of a person, which occur further on.

[80] The Mlechhas intended here are probably the Greeks: *vide* Lassen, *Ind. Alt* (2nd ed.) vol. II. p. 285.

APPENDIX X

A NOTE ON KALHANA'S *RAJATARNGINI*

By R. C. Dutt

The history of Kashmir ... commences at the time of the Kuru War. Fortunately we are able to fix this date with a greater degree of certainty than we can fix the dates of most other events of ancient Hindu history. A number of very distinguished scholars, starting from different premises, and proceeding by different lines of argument, both astronomical and chronological, have yet arrived at much the same conclusion, *viz.*, that the Kuru war and the final compilation of the Vedas took place about the 12th or 14th century before Christ. We need not here recapitulate their researches and reasoning on this point, but will only briefly allude to the results. Colebrooke, following two different lines of reasoning, arrives nevertheless, at the same date, *viz.* 14th century before Christ. Wilford fixes 1370 B. C. while Hamilton puts it down to the 12th century B. C. Archdeacon Pratt accepts the conclusion of Colebrooke. All later historians and scholars have accepted either the 14th or the 12th century before Christ as the date of the momentous events which opened a new epoch in the history of India.

To the results of the researches of these eminent scholars we will only add the testimony of such facts and figures as the history of two great kingdoms in India can supply. The History of Magadha, thanks to the Buddhistic revolution, presents us with some dates which cannot be disputed. Sakya Sinha, the founder of the Buddhist religion, died about 550 B. C., and thirty-five princes reigned in Magadha between the Kuru war and the time of Sakya Sinha. Seventeen or sixteen years are considered a good general average of the reigns of kings in India; we shall accept the more moderate average, *viz*, 16 years, and this calculation shows that the Kuru war took place in the 12th century before Christ.

Last, though not the least, is the testimony of the history of Kashmir. Kalhana Pandit, the writer of the history, lived in

[1] (1848—1909) A distinguished ex-Member of the Indian Civil Service and President, Indian National Congress, Lucknow, 1899.

1148 A. D. and his dates are perfectly reliable, and have rightly been accepted by H. H. Wilson, up to five or six centuries previous to the time of the historian. Indeed there can be no doubt as to the correctness of Kalhana's dates up to the reign of Durlabhabardhana, who ascended the throne in 598 A. D.[2] When, however the historian travels to an interior period, his dates become extravagant and unreliable, and require to be adjusted. Wilson has, by so adjusting the dates, ascertained that the reign of Gonanda I, who was contemporaneous with the heroes of the Kuru war, happened about 1400 B. C. We should have very much liked to see Dutt attempting such an adjustment of dates. Since, however, he has not done so, and, as we cannot for many reasons accept Wilson's dates,[3] we shall attempt to adjust the dates for ourselves. (See J. C. Dutt : *Kings of Kashmira*)

We have seen that Durlabhabardhana ascended the throne in 598 A. D. Thirty-seven kings reigned between the time of Gonanda III and Durlabhabardhana. Giving sixteen years to each reign, we find that Gonanda III ascended the throne A. D. 6, that is about the commencement of the Christian era.

What was the period which elapsed between Gonanda I and Gonanda III? We are told that fifty-two kings reigned from Gonanda I and Gonanda III, and they reigned over a period if 1266 years. This gives an average of over twenty-four years for each reign, which, though not impossible, is highly improbable.

[2] Wilson makes it 615 A. D. But we accept the dates given by J. C. Dutt (*Kings of Kashmira*), because his work is a literal translation of the Sanskrit history, whereas Wilson often consulted Persian authorities in writing his essay. The difference, however, is only of seventeen years.

[3] Wilson gives 20 years to each religion which is too high an average to lead to a correct conclusion. According to his calculation again, the date of disputes between Buddhists and Brahmans in Kashmir is anterior to the birth of Sakya Sinha, the founder of Buddhism, which is absurd. Lastly, he makes the curious mistake of supposing that the first fifty-two kings of Kashmir, whose names have mostly been lost, were anterior to Gonanda I. whereas the following passages from the *Rajatarangini* clearly shows that the fifty-two kings whose names have mostly been lost were Gonanda I. and his successors down to Abhimanyu. "No mention is made of fifty-two kings on account of their irreligion. Four of these, Gonanda, &c are named by Nilamuni ; Padma Mihira, following Halaraja, gives an account of eight kings (descendants of Asoka) from Lava ; and Srichchhavillake speaks of five only. He writes 'from Asoka to Abhimanyu, five kings have been named out of fifty-two"—J. C. Dutt's Translation. We are much afraid Wilson's Persian authorities led him into these and similar mistakes...

Either, then, the period (1266 years) has been wrongly described, or there is a mistake in the number given of the kings who reigned in this period. If we had as clear and reliable an account of these fifty-two kings before Gonanda III, as we have of the kings who succeeded him, who should not have hesitated to give them each an average of sixteen years' reign as we have done to the successors of Gonanda III. and so reduced the alleged period of 1266 years to 832 years. But so far from having any reliable account of these fifty-two kings, the very names of most of them are lost, and we have therefore the bare assertion of Kalhana that fifty-two unknown kings reigned. It is more than probable therefore that, in reckoning this number, weak princes who reigned for short periods have not been included and that the actual number of kings who reigned before Gonanda III. was over fifty-two. That this is likely, appears from a disagreement between two authorities whom Kalhana quotes in his history. Padmamihira says there were eight kings from Lava to Abhimanyu, while Srichchhavillaka says there were only five. It is clear, therefore, that no reliance can be placed on the number given of the princes who reigned before Gonanda III. It is very likely that the number was over fifty-two, and it is not unlikely therefore that the period covered by these reigns has correctly been described as 1266 years.

Even assuming that only fifty-two princes did reign from Gonanda I to Gonanda III, it is not impossible to suppose that the average of their reigns was twenty-four years, and that they ruled for 1266 years, which is the period given by Kalhana. We cannot therefore be far from the truth if we accept Kalhana's statement that 1266 years elapsed from the reign of Gonanda I, to that of Gonanda III. But we have seen before that Gonanda III began to reign in 6 A. D. It follows, therefore, that Gonanda I. reigned and the heroes of the Kuru war lived, in 1260 B. C. Such is the testimony borne by the history of Kashmir as regards the date of the war of the Kurus.

Thus, then, by the concurrent testimony of all antiquarians and schoars of note who have enquired into the subject, by reasoning based on astronomical, philological and chronological premises, as well as by the evidence afforded by the histories of Maghada and of Kashmir respectively, the date of the war of the Kurus is fixed between the 12th and the 14th century before Christ. This is the date when the Vedic period closed and the Vedas were arranged and compiled, and a new epoch in the history of India was opened. And this, too, is the date from which the history of Kashmir commences. From this date then, shall we follow Kalhana's history of Kashmir occassionally alluding to contemporaneous events which transpired in other parts of Inia.

Gonanda I. then reigned about 1260 B.C. and was the friend of Jarasandha and the opponent of Krishna. He invaded Mathura, the capital of Krishna, but was defeated in battle and fell pierced with wounds. The proud heart of Damodara I. brooded over the circumstances of his father's death, and determined to wipe out the disgrace, and he suddenly attacked Krishna in the midst of some nuptial festivities on the banks of the Indus. Krishna, however, was victorious, and Damodar, like his father, fell on the field of battle. His widow Yasabati was with child, and was raised to the throne. In due time, she gave birth to a boy who was named after his grandfather Gonanda. It was in the reign of the boy Gonanda II, that the war of the Kurus was fought, but Gonanda II was only a boy and would not join either side. Then there is a long blank in the history of Kashmir, and nothing is known of the successors of Gonanda II for several centuries. Indeed the eventful period which elapsed from the war of the Kurus to the rise of Buddhism in India is a blank in the history of Kashmir.

But although this is a blank period in Kashmirian history, it is not a blank in the great story of the progress of the Hindu nation and civilisation. On the contrary, we know with some degree of accuracy, the sort of change which Hindu society underwent during the centuries after the Kuru war. The Kshatriyas, or warrior caste, of King Janaka's time had asserted their equality with Brahmans or priests in learning and in rank, and the successors of Janaka had signalised their prowess by carrying the Aryan banner to the southermost point of India, as also by fighting the great war subsequently described in the Mahabharata. This activity of the Kshattriyas manifested itself no less in bold investigations into philosophy and religion than in wars : and in the Upanishads, composed about this time, very often by Kshatriyas, we see the first recorded human attempts to solve those problems of philosophy which ages and centuries after puzzled the thinkers of Greece, Arabia or modern Europe.

But this activity of the Kshatriyas appears to have abated after a time, and the Brahmans succeeded in assuming and even monopolising, that supremacy in thought and learning which the warriors had in vain tried to share with them. In the *Sutra* literature, which was written after the Vedic period, we mark not only the activity of the Brahminical intellect, but also that unquestioned supremacy which the priests at last established over the Kshatriyas. Not only were philosophy, astronomy, rhetoric, grammar, metre and cognate sciences cultivated by Brahmans with wonderful acuteness and success, but social laws were laid down investing Brahmans with a halo of unapproachable sanctity and glory. Indeed Brahmans appear to have used the power which they had now attained to their best advantage; there was one law for them, another law for others; Brahman offenders were treated with leniency, offenders against Brahmans were punished with tenfold severity; Brahmans alone had the right to expound the Vedas; they alone performed all ceremonies and received gifts from other castes; they monopolised all the highest and most honourable executive and judicial posts under government, and they also enjoyed a practical monopoly of philosophy, science and learning. However much we may admire the genius of the Brahmans of this period; however highly we may esteem their six schools of philosophy their astronomy, their science and their poetry;—the Ramayana and the Mahabharata were originally composed at this period,—we nevertheless cannot help deploring the loss of that equality between man and man which the Kshatriyas had vainly attempted to establish, and we deeply regret the civilisation of this period in which the rights of humanity were sacrificed in order to add to the priviledges and heighten the dignity of priests and priesthood.

Happily the Kshatriyas made another attempt to shake off priestly supremacy and preach the equality of man, and the effect was the rise of that religion which even now, after the lapse of over two thousand years, counts a larger portion of the human race among its followers than either Christianity, or Muhammadanism, or Hinduism or any other religion. This reaction against priestly supremacy, this second recorded attempt of Kshatriyas to proclaim the equality of man is known as the rise of Buddhism in the sixth century before Christ.

We need not here retrace the story of the great Sakya Sinha and his religion, which ignored caste inequalities and proclaimed the equality of man and humanity towards all living beings. India listened to the great lesson and benefited by it, and the great religious revolution evoked a social and a political change. Extension of ideas had its effect on the political economy of India, and the supremacy of King Asoka and of the Buddhist religion over all northern India, in the third century before Christ, was only an effect of the great lessons and the enlarged views which Sakya Sinha had preached to the world. For two or three centuries more Buddhism remained the dominant religion in India, after which it gradually gave place to that Brahmanism and priestly supremacy which prevails to the present day. Let us, then, turn to the history of Kashmir and see whether we discover here that contention between Brahmanism and Buddhism which shook all India for centuries before and after the birth of Christ.

After the long blank which we have spoken of above, we come to a line of eight kings, from Lava to Sachinara, of whom Kalhana has very little to say. Sachinara was succeeded by Asoka, who was the fifth prince before Gonanda III and who, therefore, according to our calculation, reigned in the first century before Christ. Buddhism was then the prevailing religion in India; and Kalhana tells us that Asoka himself was a Buddhist and a truthful and a spotless king, and built many Buddhist stupas on the banks of the Bitasta (Jhelum.) He also built a *chaitya* so high that its top could not be seen, and he founded the city of Srinagar which exists to the present day. He also, according to Kalhana, pulled down the wall of an old Hindu temple and built a new wall to it; and the writer of the *Ayin-i-Akbari* is therefore probably right in saying that Asoka "abolished the Brahminical rites and substituted those of Jaina."[4] There can be no doubt, therefore, that the dispute between Brahmans and Buddhists had commenced before the time of Asoka, and that in the first century before Christ Buddhism was the prevailing religion in Kashmir, as elsewhere in India.

The death of Asoka appears to have been a serious loss to Buddhism in Kashmir, for his successor Jaloka appears to have been a Hindu and a Saiva. He was a powerful king and drove back the Mlechchhas (Scythians?) who had overrun Kashmir during the lifetime of his father and he extended his conquests to the eastern side of Kanouj. This conquest of one of the great centres of Brahmanism by a prince of Kashmir "possibly marks[5] the introduction of the Brahmanical creed in its more perfect form into the kingdom" of Kashmir. Kalhana informs us that from Kanouj, Jaloka carried to his kingdom some men of each of the four castes who were versed in law and religion, (Brahmanical of course,) that he created new offices after the orthodox method, that he established eighteen places of worship,

[4] H. H. Wilson, *Asiatic Researches*, Vol. XV.
[5] Ibid.

and used to hear the *Nandi Purana* recited. The triumph of Brahmanism seemed to be complete, but the Buddhists did not lose heart, and their attempts to win over the king have been thus handed down by tradition in the shape of a tale. We quote from Dutt's translation :

"It is narrated of this king that one day, when he was going to the temple of Vijayeshvara, he met a woman in the way who asked him for some food, and when he promised her whatever food she wanted, she changed herself into some deformed shape and asked for human flesh. Unwilling to kill any one to satisfy her unnatural appetite, he permitted her to take off what she liked from his own body. This heroic self-devotion seemed to move her, and she remarked, that for his tender regard for the life of others she considered him a second Buddha. The king, being a follower of Shiva, did not know Buddha, and asked her who Buddha was, whom she took him to be. She then unfolded her mission and said, that on the other side of the hill of Lokaloka, where the sun never shone, there lived a tribe of Krittika who were the followers of Buddha. 'This tribe', she continued with the eloquence of a missionary, 'were never angry even with those who did them injury, forgave them that trespassed against them, and even did them good. They taught truth and wisdom to all, and were willing to dispel the darkness of ignorance that covered the earth. But this people,' she added, 'you have injured. There was a monastery belonging to us in which the beating of drums once disturbed your sleep, and incited by the advice of wicked men, you have destroyed the monastery. The angry Buddhists sent me to murder you, but our high priest interfered ; he told me that you were a powerful monarch, against whom we would not be able to cope. He said that if you would listen to me, and built a monastery with your gold, you would atone for the sins of which you are guilty in destroying the former one. Here I came, therefore and tested your heart in disguise., Krittidevi then returned to her people after extorting from the king a promise to build a monastery, and agreeably to his promise he caused it to be erected on the very place of their meeting."

Jaloka was succeeded by Damodara II, and in the occount of his reign we have the counterpart of the story we have given above. For now it was the Brahmans who were angry with the king, probably for his favouring Buddhism, and their attempt to revive their faith is thus handed down by tradition in the shape of a tale which we also quote from Dutt's work :

"One day, when tht king was going to bathe, previous to performing a Sraddha, some hungry Brahmans asked him for food; but he disregarded their request and was proceeding to the river, when the Brahmans by force of their worship brought the river to his feet. 'Look' said they, 'here is Bitasta (Jhelum), now feed us!" But the king suspected it to be the effect of magic. 'Go away for the present,' replied the king. 'I will not feed you till I have bathed'. The Brahmans then cursed him saying that he would be turned into a serpent. When much entreated to withdraw their curse, they so far mitigated it as to say, that if the king could listen to the *Ramayana* from the beginning to the end in one day, he would be restored to his form. To this day he may be seen running about at Damodarasuda in the form of a thirsty serpent.'

These stories, which appear so childish on the face of them, are simply invaluable when taken according to their proper significance. They show that in the first century before Christ the great religious revolution which had shaken the whole continent of India had also found its way into the secluded heights of Kashmir, and that Brahmans and Buddhists in that country were struggling for that supremacy which eventually crowned the efforts of the latter.

Such Brahman supremacy, however, was not achieved in a day, and in the joint reigns of Hushka, Jushka and Kanishka, the immediate successors of Damodara II, Buddhism was once more triumphant, and "during their long reign Buddhist hermits were all powerful in the country and Buddhist religion prevailed without opposition".[6] In the reign of their successor, Abhimanyu, "the Buddhists, under their great leader Nagarjuna, continued to gain strength in the country; they not only defeated in argument the Pandits who upheld the worship of Siva, and rejected the duties prescribed in the *Nila Purana*, but had the influence to discontinue the ceremonies and worship enjoined by it. The Nagas, in consequence, rose in arms, murdered many people, mostly Buddhists, by rolling down ice from the mountains, and carried on their devastations year by year.[7] Thus religious differences, as elsewhere, culminated in civil war, man killed man for differences in belief and the country was in confusion. Brahman intellect and influence prevailed in the end over Buddhism, and Chandracharya, the learned and noted grammarian,

[6] Rajatarangini,—Dutt's Translation.

[7] Ibid.

led the van of Brahmanical success. It was by the instrumentality of such powerful intellects which appeared in India from time to time, that Brahmanism slowly triumphed over Buddhism from the commencement of the Christian era. Chandracharya, of Kashmir, was probably the first of these apostles of modern Brahmanism ; Sankaracharya, of Southern India, who lived and preached in the 8th or 9th century after Christ, was the last. Abhimanyu was the last of his dynasty. His successor, Gonanda III., began a new dynasty in 6 A. D., as we have seen before.

Here we come across a curious test by which we may examine the correctness or otherewise of the dates we have given to the reigns of kings. The Chinese traveller Hieun Tsiang tells us that Kanishka succeeded to the kingdom of Kashmir "in the fourhundredth year after the Nirvana." (Beales' translation). R. Davids fixes the Nirvana at about 412 B. C. So that Kanishka began his reign about the beginning of the Christian era. The profound antiquarian Lassen also proves from coins that Kanishka lived between 10 A. D., and 40 A. D. Accepting this conclusion as correct, and giving 16 years for the intervening reign of Abhimanyu, we find that Gonanda III. commenced his reign at 56 A. D., i. e., just half a century after the date that we have given him. If then, in testing our long chain of calculations and dates by a random and severe test, an one single point we find that we are out only by 50 years, it follows that the chain of our calculations cannot be very far from correct.

There is yet another fact about Kanishka which we wish to mention before we proceed further with our story. Indian writers have carefully concealed the fact of foreign immigrations and conquests in India though we know such things have taken place. The present instance is a case in point. Kalhana suppresses the fact that Kanishka was a foreign invader. We learn from the Chinese historians however that he belongs to the Gushan tribe of the Yuei-Chi, who came originally from the borders of China. We learn from Hieun Tsiang that tributary princes from China sent hostages to him, and that the town where the hostages resided was called Chinapati....

The fifth king after Gonanda III. was Nara I, who "burnt thousands and thousands of monasteries and gave to the Brahmans who dwelt at Madhyamata the villages that supported those monasteries". The reason assigned for this conduct is, that a Buddhist had eloped with the king's wife ; but this seems unlikely and false, and has apparently been got up by later Brahamans to blacken the character of the Buddhists. The real cause seems to be, that, in the struggle between Brahamanism and Buddhism, the former had now gained complete ascendancy, and the gradual extinction of Buddhism in Kashmir was only a question of time.

The fifth king after Nara I. was Mukula, in whose reign Mlechchhas (Schthians?) once more overran Kashmir. His successor, Mihirakula, is described as a powerful but cruel king, and is said to have invaded and conquered Ceylon and then returned through Chola, Karnata, Nata and other kingdoms. Gopaditya was the sixth king after Mihirakula, and he bestowed many villages on Brahmans, expelled from his country irreligious Brahmans who used to eat garlic, brought purer Brahmans from foreign countries, and forbade the slaughter of animals except for religious purposes. Brahmanism in Kashmir, as elsewhere in India, was apparenty assuming its most rigid shape after its triumph over Buddhism; priests invented new laws and prohibitions to enslave a superstitious people; thought and culture were prohibited to all except Brahmans, apparently to prevent any future reaction against Brahman supremacy; gods and religious rites and superstitious observances were multiplied by a number of modern Puranas, written by astute priests, but prudently ascribed to the great Vyasa the compiler of the Vedas, and the unhealthy and demoralizing religion, Puranism, fast reared its head over the ashes of Buddhism. The nation which had once dared to question the supremacy of Brahmans and Brahmanism was now shakled by its chains, once and for ever.

Three kings reigned after Gopaditya, after which Pratapaditya began a new dynasty in the year 342 A. D. according to our calculation. A severe famine visited Kashmir in the reign of Tunjina I, the grandson of Pratapaditya and the son and successor of Jalauka, in consequence of the *sali* grain being blighted by a sudden and heavy frost. The king died childless, and Vijaya, of a different family, succeeded him. Jayendra, his son, reigned after him, and after him his minister, Sandhimati, became king, but resigned the high office in favour of Meghabahana, a descendant from the older royal dynasty of Gonanda III.

Meghabahana, who ascended the throne in 438 A. D. according to our calculation, seemed to have been favourably inclined towards Buddhism, and his queens built numerous Buddhist monasteries in the kingdom. Following the Buddhist doctrines, the king not only prohibited the slaughter of animals in his own kingdom, but is said to have "carried his arms to the sea, and even to Ceylon, making the subdued kings promise not to kill animals." Meghabahana was succeeded by his son, Shreshtasena, and his son, Hiranya, succeeded him.

After the death of Hiranya, a foreigner, Matrigupta, obtained the kingdom of Kashmir by the help of Bikramaditya, king of Ojein.[8] This was probably the great Bikramaditya of Ojein in whose reign the poet Kalidasa lived (5th century A. D.), but the historians of Kashmir mistakes him for Bikramaditya, the foe of the Sakas, who lived in the first century before Christ.[9] Matrigupta was a courtier of Bikramaditya, and, was rewarded by him with the kingdom of Kashmir ; and the people of Kashmir accepted the king sent to them by the renowned king of Ojein.

In the meantime Pravarasena, the nephew of the late king Hiranya, and the rightful heir of Kashmir, marched against Bikramaditya who had usurped his heritage and bestowed it on a stranger. Bikramaditya died about this time, and his protege, Matrigupta, resigned in grief, and Pravarasena, therefore, easily got back the kingdom of his uncle. He was a powerful prince and defeated the people of Saurastra (near Surat), and seven times defeated Siladitya, the successor of Bikramaditya of Ojein, and brought away from that place the ancient throne of Kashmir, which Bikramaditya appears to have taken away from Kashmir. His son, Yudhistira II, and grandson, Narendraditya, succeeded him in their turns, and the latter was succeeded by his brother, Ranaditya. Bikramaditya, the son of Ranaditya, was a powerful king, and so was his brother and successor, Baladitya, with whom the dynasty ended. Baladitya died 598 A. D. and his son-in-law Durlabhabardhana, of Kayastha caste, began a new dynasty. From this date, 598 A. D. we can rely on Kalhana's dates ...

Durlabhabardhana was succeeded by his son Durlabhaka, in 634 A. D., and his son Chandrapira, succeeded in 684 A. D. Chandrapira was murdered by his brother Tarapira, who employed some Brahmans to do this foul deed, in 693, but the impious brother, after a short reign of four years, himself fell a victim to the intrigue of Brahmans and was murdered. His brother

[8] Modern Ujjain.

[9] This is the one great reason of the confusion of Kalhana's dates. His dates are quite reliable from his own time 1148 A. D. to the reign of Durlabhabardhana 598 A. D. Only six kings ruled between Durlabhabardhana and Matrigupta ; and, as Kalhana believed Matrigupta to be contemporaneous with Bikramaditya of the Saka era, i. e. of the first century before Christ, he makes these six kings reign over the whole of the intermediate six centuries ; Hence Kalhana's dates are perfectly useless for the period anterior to 598 A. D.

Lalitaditya succeeded in 697 A. D. and was a powerful and warlike king, and set out on an expedition to subdue the continent. He subdued Kanyakubja, and Bhababhuti, the greatest dramatic poet of India after Kalidasa, came over to the court of the conqueror. He then proceeded on his march of conquest through Kalinga, Gour, and along the Bay of Bengal to Karnata, which was at that time governed by a powerful queen. She submitted to Lalitaditya, who is said to have then "crossed the sea, passing from one island to another". Then the king turned northwards, crossed the Vindya and entered Avanti.

Some hard fighting followed, when the king tried to subdue the hardy races and kings of the country now called Rajputana, after which the king returned to his country. He built numerous edifices, Buddhist as well as Brahmanical, and his queens and ministers followed his example. In the end the king appears to have lost his life in attempting to penetrate the Himalayas to conquer the unknown North.

Kubalayapira succeeded his father in 733 A. D., but had to resign in favour of his more powerful brother Bajraditya who reigned from 734 to 741 A. D. We read that "this luxurious king had many females in his zenana. He sold many people to the Mlechchhas and introduced their evil habits." Who are these Mlechchhas, with their luxurious and evil habits, and their custom of buying slaves in India, of whom we now hear for the first time? The dates at once show that they were Muhammad Kasim, the first Mahomedan invader of India and his successors, who kept possession of Scinde from 711 to 750 A. D. The passage above quoted, then, is the first mention of Mahomedans in the history of Kashmir, unless some of the victories of Lalitaditya of which we have spoken in the last paragraph, were victories over the Mahomedans of Scinde.[10]

[10] Thus we are told that Lalitaditya, after crossing over to the north of the Vindya mountains, "thrice defeated Dassani and subdued him. He then conquered the Bouttas, in whose naturally pale faces no further sign of anxiety was visible. He also conquered Darad". Dussani is not improbably a corruption of a Mahomedan name, while the pale-faced race may have been the fair countrymen of Mahomed Kasim. Then again we read that "to mark his conquests he (Lalitaditya) obliged other kings to wear a symbol of subjection, which they bear to this day. The Turashkas commemorate the fact of their being bound, by generally clasping both their hands behind their backs and shaving the front part of their heads." Who were the Turashkas subdued by Lalitaditya unless they were the Mahomedan Turks of Scind? Lastly, we are told, that

Prithivyapira reigned for four years, and Sangramapira for seven days, after which the powerful Jayapira ascended the throne in 754 and reigned for thirty-one years. He was a great patron of learning, invited men of genius to his court, and employed learned men in collecting the fragments of Patanjali's works, and Commentary on Katyana's Notes on Panini's grammar. These are the greatest grammarians of India, and we know from the above passage that they must have lived long before the eighth century of the Christian era. Jayapira travelled out of his kingdom in disguise to Gour, there married the king's daughter, and, returning to his country, vanquished and killed his rebellious brother-in-law, who had usurped Kashmir in his absence. Soon after he again set out for conquest. In the kingdom of Bhimsena, and again in Nepal, he was beaten and imprisoned, but on both occasions he managed to escape and to triumph over his enemies in the end.

Returning to his country, Jayapira followed the advice of Kayastha ministers and financiers, and so offended the Brahmans, who (being the historians of Kashmir) have not failed to heap abuse on him. The following account of the death of Jayapira, which we take from Dutt's translation, will give a good idea of the insolence and pride of the Brahmans, as well as of the manner in which they fabricated stories and interwove them with history in order to preserve their supremacy and glorify their power.

"The Brahmanas who dwelt at Tulamula, once came to say something to the king, but were struck in his presence by his door-keeper, and consequently were very angry. 'Brahmans were never insulted before, even in the presence of Manu, Mandhata, Rama and other great kings,' they said, 'and when angry they can destroy in a moment the heaven with Indra, the earth with her mountains, and the nether world with its Naga-chief'. The king, who would not ask for avdice, and was deserted by his feudatory kings, replied with supercilious pride : 'You cunning people who eat by begging, what pride is this of yours that you pretend to do what the Rishis did'. The Brahmanas were cowed down by his frown, but one Iitti thus replied :—'We conduct ourselves according to the times ; as you are a king, even so we are Rishis'. The king scornfully enquired : 'Art thou the great Rishi,

the "king of the sandy Sindhu sent a messenger to beguile the king of Kashmir and so make him and his men perish in the desert ; but that the king overcame all obstacles and "defeated the wily king of Sindhu", and devastated his country.

Vishvamitra, or Vashishta, or Agastha?' And, as if flaming with anger, the other replied, 'If you be Harishchandra, Trishanku or Nahusha, then I am one of those you mention. The king then answered with a smile, 'The curse of Vishvamitra and others destroyed Harishchandra, &c., what will your anger effect?' The Brahmana struck the earth with his hand and said, 'Will not my anger bring down Brahmadanda on thee? Then said the angry king, 'Let fall the Brahmadanda, why delay it longer?' "O cruel man! there it falls.' And no sooner had Iitti said so, than a golden bar from the canopy fell on the king. The wound degenerated into erysipelatous inflammation, and insects generated on the suppuration. He suffered great pain, the sample of what he would have to suffer in hell. After five nights, he who had courted danger, died."

His son, Lalitapira, reigned for twelve years and was succeeded by his half-brother, Sangramapira, who reigned till 795 A.D. On his death, Chippatajayapira, the son of Lalitapira by a concubine, was raised to the throne, and the five brothers of this woman shared all the ruling power among themselves. They and their sons successively set up three more kings on the throne, after which Avantivarma, the grandson of one of these brothers, ascended the throne, and thus commenced a new dynasty in 885 A. D.

It is in the reign of Avantivarma that we first read an account of the country being improved by drainage and irrigation operations, and Suyya was the great enginneer who performed this work. He was of low birth, and as usual, his attempts have been somewhat grotesquely described; but nevertheless, our readers will not fail to observe from the following passage that Kashmir was greatly benefited by the industry and intellect of this great man. We quote from Dutt's translation.

"One day, when some people were grieving on account of the recent floods, he, Suyya , remarked that he had intellect but not money, and he could therefore give no redress. This speech was reported to the king by his spies, and the king wondered and caused him to be brought before him. The king asked him as to what he said. He fearlessly repeated that he had intellect but no money. The courtiers pronounced him to be mad, but the king, in order to try his intellect, placed all his wealth at the disposal of this man. Suyya took out many vessels filled with dinnaras, but went by boat to Madava. There in the village named Nandaka, which was under water, he threw a pot of dinnaras, and returned. Although the courtiers pronounced him to be undoubtedly mad, the king heard of his work, and enquired as to what he did afterwards. At Yakshadara in Kramarajya he began to throw dinnaras by handfuls into the water. The Vitasta was there obstructed by rocks which had fallen into its bed from both its rocky banks; and the villagers who were suffering from scarcity, began to search for the dinnaras, and in so doing removed the rocks which were in the bed of the river and cleared the passage of the water. No sooner had the water flowed out than Suyya raised a stone embankment along the Vitasta, which was completed within seven days. He then cleared the bed of the river, and then broke down the embankments. The passage was now quite open, and the river flowed easily and rapidly towards the sea, as if anxiously and eagerly, after this long detention; and consequently the land again appeared above the waters. He then cut new canals from the Vitasta wherever he thought that the course of the river had been obstructed. Thus many streams issued out of one main river, even like the several heads of a serpent from one trunk. Sindhu which flowed from Trigrama to the left, and Vitasta on the right, were made to meet one another at Vainyasvami. And even to this day the junction made by Suyya, near this town, exists; as also the two gods Vishnusvami and Vainyasvami at Phalapura and Parihasaura situated on either side of the junction; and the god Hrishikesha whom Suyya worshipped, just at the junction. And to this day may also be seen the trees which grew on the banks of the river as it flowed before, distinguished by marks of ropes by which boats were tied to them. Thus Suyya diverted the course of rivers. He raised a stone embankment seven *yojanas* in length; and thereby brought the waters of the Mahapadma lake under control. He joined the waters of the lake Mahapadma with those of the Vitasta, and built many populous villages after having rescued the land from the waters....He examined several places and irrigated many villages (the produce of which did not depend on rain) by means of artificial canals cut from the Chanula and other rivers until the whole country became beautiful. Thus Suyya benefited the country such as even Kashyapa and Valadeva had not done".

Avantivarma died in 883, the first Vaishnava king that we read of. Vaishnavism and Saktaism are later phases of Hinduism than Shaivaism, and in the history of Kashmir we scarcely hear anything of Vaishnavism till the present time (1880).

His successor Sankaravarma, was a great conqueror and conquered Guzerat. Returning to his country, he listened to the advice of his Kayastha financiers and imposed taxes on the people which made him unpopular with them, or any rate, with the offended Brahmans who narrate his history. He conquered many hill places on the banks of the Indus and was at last killed by the arrow of a hunter. Surendravati and two other queens perished with him on the pyre, 902 A. D.

In the short reign of his successor Gopalavarma, the minister Prabhakara (who was a favourite of the queen mother Sugandha), defeated "the reigning Shahi" because he had disobeyed his orders to build a town in "Shahirajya". This seems to have been some petty dependent or tributary king, and we shall hereafter read more of the "Shahirajya".

Gopalavarma's brother, Sankata, dying ten days after the former, their mother Sugandha, a dissolute woman, reigned for two years by the help of the Ekangas. The Tantri infantry, however, raised Partha to the throne; a civil war ensued, the Ekangas were beaten and the queen Sugandha killed, 906 A. D. The Tantris, being now supreme, set up one king after another, according as they were bribed and courted, until Chakravarma with the help of the Damaras and Ekangas at last broke their power in 935 A. D., and for the third time ascended the throne. Within two years he was assassinated by some Damaras and was succeeded by Partha's son, Unmattavanti. This young man killed his father, but died soon after, and his successor Suravarma was the last of this unfortunate dynasty which ended in 939 A. D.

Yasaskara, the first king of the new dynasty, was the son of Prabhakara, who had been minister of Gopalavarma of the preceding dynasty, and was famed for his justice; but in the very year of his death Purbagupta murdered his son, Sangarma, and founded a new dynasty. His son, Kshemagupta, inherited the vices and dissolute habits of his father and reigned eight years. His son Abhimanyu, was the only virtuous and worthy king of the line, and reigned fourteen years; and on his death his mother, Didda (widow of Kshemagupta), successively murdered three infant kings (her grandsons), Nandigupta, Tribhubanagupta, and Bhimagupta, and became queen in 980 A. D. She reigned for 23 years, and in her reign her favourite, Tunga, defeated the king of Rajapuri.

Didda's nephew, Kshamapati, ascended the throne in 1003 A. D. and reigned till 1028 A. D. Tunga, who had been the favourite of Didda, was all powerful during the reign of her nephew, and went out with a Kashmirian army and Rajput and other subsidiary forces to help the Shahi king against the attack of the Turashkas. We shall quote Kalhana's account of the event from Dutt's translation :

"The Kashmirians crossed the river Toushi, and destroyed the detachment of soldiers sent by Hammira to reconnoitire. But though the Kashmirians were eager for the fight, the wise Shahi repeatedly advised them to take shelter behind the rock, but Tungga disregarded the advice, for all advice is vain when one is doomed to destruction. The general of the Turks was well versed in the tactics of war and brought out his army early in the morning. On this the army of Tungga immediately dispersed, but the troops of the Shahi fought for a while."

The heroism of the Shahi king, however, was unavailing. He was beaten, and his kingdom was destroyed for ever.

Now who was the Hammira (a Mahomedan name apparently) and who were these powerful Turashkas who defeated the Kashmirians and the Rajputs and annexed the "Shahirajya," and ally or dependent of Kashmir? The dates show at once that Kalhana is speaking of the invasion of India by the invincible Mahmud of Ghuzni.[11]

Tunga was soon after murdered, and Nandimukha was sent with another army against the Turashkas, but they, too, fled back to their country before the conquering Moslems.

Hariraja succeeded his father, Kshamapati, and reigned only for 22 days, after which his brother, Ananta Deva, ascended the throne and reigned 35 years years, i. e. from 1028 to 1063 A. D. We read that in this reign one Brahmaraja combined with seven Mlechchha kings had entered Kashmir, but was beaten back by Rudrapala, the powerful Kashmirian general. When we remember that, from the time of Mahmud of Ghuzni, a part of the Punjab always remained under Mahommedan rule, we are at no loss to guess who these seven Mlechchhas were.

After a long reign of 35 years Ananta was prevailed upon by his queen to resign in favour of his son Ranaditya ; but the prince was unworthy of their confidence, and shocked his parents and all men by his excesses of wickedness, folly and dissipation. Disheartened at this conduct of their son, the aged parents retired to Bijayeswara and passed their days in devotion, but even there they were not allowed to enjoy repose. Harassed by

[11] Hammira was therefore either a general of Mahmud, or was the great conqueror himself, "well versed" indeed "in the tactics of war"! The letters *r* and *d* are interchangeable ; and if we eliminate the first syllable of Mahammud, we get the Sanscritized name Hammira.

the enmity of this ungrateful son, Ananta at last committed suicide, and his widow ascended the funeral pyre.

The ingratitude of Ranaditya towards his father was punished by the misconduct of his son, Harsha, who rose in rebellion. Ranaditya died in 1089 A. D., a victim to his dissolute habits; his son Utkarsha succeeded him, but was soon deposed by his abler and more popular brother, Harsha, and committed suicide. Bijayamalla, who had helped his brother Harsha to the throne, now thirsted for the kingdom himself, but the fraternal war finally came to an end by the accidental death of Bijaymalla.

Harsha's powerful general, Kandarpa, subdued the king of Rajapuri, but at last retired from the court in disgust at the growing jealousy of the king. Harsha subsequently attempted to subdue Rajapuri and Darad respectively but failed in both his attempts. His excessive taxation and his oppression over the Damaras made them rise in rebellion; and they had powerful chiefs in two brothers Uchchala and Sussala. Uchchala defeated the Lord of Maudala, but was subsequently beaten by the royal army.

His brother Sussala defeated the royal commander Manikya, broke through all opposition and defeated the Lord of Mandala, but was at last beaten by Bhoja, the son of king Harsha. At last Uchchala defeated Harsha and his son Bhoja in a single battle, burnt the capital and became king. The unfortunate Harsha retired to the tent of a hermit, but was there traced out and killed, 1101 A. D.

We have only one more remark to make of Harsha's reign. Allusions to Turashkas and their kingdom become more frequent now than ever before. Thus we are told that Harsha had a hundred Turashka chiefs under his pay; that, after besieging Rajapuri, he fled back to his kingdom through fear of the Turashka who, he heard, were approaching; and lastly, that his oppressed subjects left their homes and went to the country of the Mlechchhas. Who are these Turashkas and what was their country of which we find such frequent mention during the reign of Harsha? The dates of Harsha's reign show at once that there was good reason for such frequent allusion to the rising Turashka power, for it was during Harsha's reign that Shahhabuddin Mahommed Ghori conquered Delhi, Kanouj, and the whole of northern India, and Hindu independence was lost once and for ever....

We have traced the history of Kashmir from the earliest times to the date of the final conquest of India by the

Mahomedans. We have refrained from making any remarks on the value of Kalhana's great work, because the above brief resume of it is the best commentary on its great value. We have seen how every great social or religious revolution, and every great historical event which transpired in India, have left their impress on the history of this secluded province. The history of this province has borne its testimony towards fixing the date of the great Kuru war; it has helped us to understand how Buddhism was a protest against caste distinctions, and a Kshtriya assertion of the equality of all men; it has revealed to us how Buddhism was for a time the accepted faith of the kings and peoples of India, and how, after the commencement of tht Christian era, it began to decline under the renewed exertions of Brahmans to assert their supremacy and revive their old religion. In the history of Kashmir we find evidences of the dates of the two great dramatic poets of India, viz., Kalidasa and Bhababhuti; in it we find allusions to the first Mahomedan invasion of India under the renowned Mahommed Kasim; in it we read of that "General of the Turashkas" "well versed in the tactics of war", the invincible Mahmud of Ghuzni, before whom the Kashmirian army twice recoiled in dismay and disorder and, lastly, in this history we read of the rising power and kingdom of the Turashka at the end of the eleventh century, when Delhi and Kanouj and all Northern India fell under the power of the followers of the prophet.

Such are some of the facts we learn from Kalhana's history of Kashmir, and, considering the poverty of historical records in India, the value of this record can scarcely be overestimated... —"Calcutta Review," 1880.

FINIS